"Judy Pex : with her and her husband, John, through a hunger to know the Lord in the deep places of our lives, and Judy manages to tell us how that works as she weaves her trail experiences in and out of her own life story of Jesus and His love. It is an original, gripping thing to travel with her and learn lessons of spiritual history and of how we can deepen our interior life."

**Jill Briscoe**, Author

"For thirty years I have had the incredible experience of traveling the land given to Israel by God—from Dan to Beersheba to Eilat. However, 'walking the land' with my friends Judy and John (by reading this book) has brought a whole new dimension and depth to my understanding of Israel and its people. I know you'll be enriched spiritually through Judy's story of the insights given her by her God on this journey of a lifetime."

**Kay Arthur**, PRECEPT MINISTRIES INTERNATIONAL

"I encourage you to read this book because I believe your interest in people, Israel, and God will be nurtured in an enjoyable and educational way. I was very impressed with how Judy was able to use her physical and emotional experiences as opportunities to understand Jesus (Yeshua) and learn to trust Him more than ever."

**Wayne Weissman**, Director, RAVENCREST CHALET
Member of Torchbearers International

"Reads like an adventure story. ... This book draws you, not only into their challenging journey, but also into the lives, background and values of Judy and John Pex. Along the trail are timely insertions of information about the land and peoples of Israel given in palatable proportions, enough to gain a better understanding, a fuller picture..."

**Jonathan Goldberg**, Field Leader, OM ISRAEL

*(More on next page)*

"Judy Pex is a verbal camera. She describes in such exquisite detail the vast Israeli wilderness as well as the noisy Israeli cities and towns that you feel both the concerns and the delights of such a remarkable trip. But much more, she communicates her deep love for both the land and the people, a love that accepts both the difficulties of the trail and the various and colorful individuals she and John encounter as they cross Israel from bottom to top.

"Beneath all the beauty and deeper even than Judy's appreciation for the natural wonders of Israel, is her profound and abiding faith in the One who gave both the land to that people, and the people to that land.

"I'm too old to take off like the Pexes for such an incredible adventure, but it's quite alright because I have not missed one rock, hill, or car horn—for Judy's account has guided me each step of the way along the glorious Israel Trail."

**Sam Nadler**, President, WORD OF MESSIAH
MINISTRIES, Charlotte, North Carolina


"A wonderful book. *Walk the Land* draws you into the experience of walking the Israel National Trail (*Shvil Israel*) and through this catalyst brings you shoulder to shoulder with John and Judy Pex and their Lord and Saviour, 'the Nazarene.' Through simple language a clear picture is painted that brings to life the *Shvil* and allows you to walk along with their daily progress, reflecting the real character of this warm couple. Listen to John bursting out in every chapter—irrepressible—how I envy his motivation. Judy—quietly determined and as strong as needed when it comes to the crunch. Read and enjoy solid truth, living detail. The *Shvil* trail experience is a wonderful bond that leads to far deeper and more real relationships.

**Steve Roth**, Walking/Jeep Tour Guide
and Shepherd, Upper Galilee

# WALK *the* LAND

## A Journey *on* Foot *through* Israel

# WALK *the* LAND

## A Journey *on* Foot *through* Israel

*Judith Galblum Pex*

CLADACH
Publishing

Published by
Cladach Publishing
PO Box 336144
Greeley, CO 80633
www.cladach.com

Library of Congress Control Number: 2007924907

ISBN-10: 0-97596-195-0
ISBN-13: 978-0-97596-195-7

Printed in the United States of America

# Acknowledgments

Thanks first of all to my husband, John, without whom *Walk the Land* would never have been written. He was my companion on the journey, and he supported me through every step of expressing the trip in words and bringing it into print.

Thanks to our children, Josh, Racheli, Moriah and Tom, and Yonatan, for their patience in listening and bearing with me, and for their suggestions as I explored new territory in writing and publishing a book.

Thanks to my parents, Harry and Velma Galblum, who have constantly inspired me and believed in me and were so excited about the walk and the book.

Thanks to my writers' group, Faith, Betsy, Laura, Ruth, and Zela, who have provided a sounding block. With Faith I found the courage to begin.

A few special friends encouraged me and were always available: Miriam, Pattie, and my sister Jane who contributed her expertise as a writer.

Because of wonderful editors this is a far better book than it would have been without their help. Teri went over the manuscript the first time preparing it for submission. Catherine was willing to take on this project and has done an amazing job. Hannah found the inconsistencies and noticed the small things that make a big difference.

Ultimately, God enabled me to give birth to this book as He guides me along life's paths. As God spoke to Israel, "They will neither hunger nor thirst, nor will the desert heat or the sun beat upon them. He who has compassion on them will guide them and lead them beside springs of water" (Isa. 49:10).

# TABLE OF CONTENTS

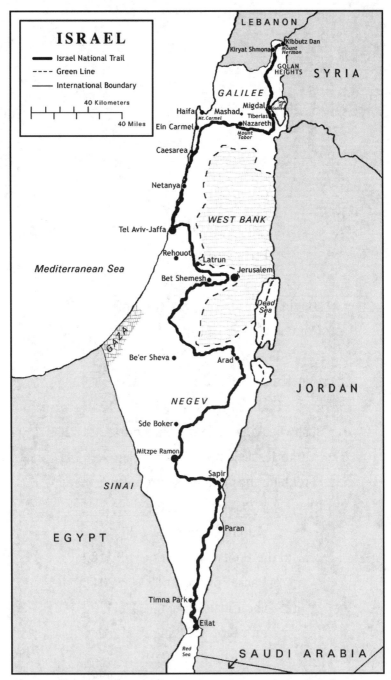

The Israel National Trail connects the best of the marked trails in Israel to create a "spinal cord" that runs the entire length of the country.

# 1. Ledges & Edges

We went to bed in the inn of Mitzpe Ramon knowing it would be wintry the next morning, with cold snapping across Israel. My imagination worked overtime as I spread our maps on the bed and contemplated setting out into unknown, apparently desolate territory. Were the two days that my husband and I had allowed for reaching our next supply station sufficient, or would we run out of food and water?

Sometimes this Israel Trail business seemed to be more than I had bargained for, but I didn't dwell on those thoughts long. I reminded myself that many people would be thankful just to get a glimpse of these biblical landscapes. Besides, we had dreamed about taking a break from our busy lives, and this was it.

At least I had no trouble falling asleep. Our seven hours of trekking across the Ramon Crater and up the edge of the cliff that day had eliminated any possibility of insomnia. But the next morning my heart was beating with trepidation as we prepared to leave Mitzpe Ramon to head east along the brink of the crater.

John and I braced ourselves against the wind as we stepped out the door of the inn into the early morning light. Mitzpe Ramon, a small town perched on the rim of the crater, was founded in the 1950s when a busload of new immigrants from Morocco was dumped in the middle of the Negev. These Jews were leaving the land where their ancestors had lived since the Spanish Inquisition of 1492; and they were returning to their biblical homeland. The new immigrants were given a few cargo containers to live in, there in the desert, and told by the Immigration Agency to found a new city. They've been struggling to do so ever since. The town subsists mainly on commerce from the nearby military bases and the traffic coming north from Eilat; however, in recent years it has been reinventing itself as a center of desert ecotourism.

Walking past children bundled in winter coats on their way to school, we were soon outside the town and hiking along the cliff, five hundred meters (or 1640 feet) above the crater floor. No matter how many times I had driven by car through the crater, I always found the view from the top breathtaking. The south rim five kilometers (or 3.1 miles) away, the multicolored sand and rock formations, and the black mounds in the middle, gave evidence of long-ago volcanic eruptions. But traveling on foot gave us a much more intimate connection with nature. The sense of awe I felt was compounded by dark clouds covering the sky and slanting streaks of rain hanging like streamers in the distance.

"Thank God the wind is behind us," John remarked.

"I honestly don't know what we'd do if we had to walk against the wind on a day like this," I said. "Think it will rain? There's rain on the horizon all around us."

"Hard to say."

This was a relatively easy trail, the jeep[1] route easier walking than a hiking path. I was glad I had brought gloves and a stocking cap. On other days we had our jackets off by now, but today we weren't even thinking of shedding them.

We fell into a steady rhythm and made good time as we continued northwest. After two hours of walking I felt a gnawing in my stomach and was ready for a snack. There was, however, no way that we could stop and eat, exposed as we were to the wind, and a light drizzle falling.

I noticed that the trail took a dip into a *wadi* (Arabic for a *stream* that is dry in the summer) up ahead and that there were bushes growing in the streambed which might provide us some protection. I was ready for my granola bar.

We had decided that on this trip we would eat only when we were hungry, but as it turned out, it was invariably *my* appetite that dictated our meal patterns.

John had no objection to a short break, though. "Too bad it didn't snow last night." He looked up at the sky and braced himself against the wind.

"Snow? I'm thankful it didn't." Dealing with cold weather had been one of my fears before we started our trip. "I hope this drizzle doesn't develop into anything stronger. Racheli sounded concerned when she called last night and said that the weather bureau was predicting snow in Mitzpe."

"Come on Jupe, why worry?" Jupe is John's Dutch nickname for me. He's the only one who calls me that. I like the way he says it. And I'll admit I like the way he is always ready for anything.

"The weather usually changes quickly around here," he added optimistically.

I, however, was remembering that when we left home we had said that the one thing which might prevent us from completing this walk would be bad weather. I knew that if it really began to rain hard we would have to stop, at least for a time. John, ever the optimist, obviously couldn't believe this drizzle might intensify and deter us.

"Can you believe we walked to Mitzpe Ramon?" John said with excitement in his voice. "Whatever else happens, no one can take that away from us." John liked to repeat this statement every time we attained another milestone, and now he said it to encourage us both.

In four hours we reached the east end of the heart-shaped crater, and the Trail made a sharp turn north, away from the edge. The wind no longer pushed us, and we immediately felt the difference.

Although the route hadn't been completely level up to this point, there hadn't been any major hills; but that all changed now. It wasn't a jeep track anymore, either. We headed up a ridge, picking our way through a field of rocks. The only trees growing in this part of the Negev Desert were down in the *wadis*, which filled up with water when it rained. Here there were only low thorny plants, hardy enough to live without rain most of the year and to withstand the incessant winds.

Our eyes were constantly on the lookout for the Israel Trail signs: three parallel white, blue, and orange painted stripes. The signs weren't always in obvious places, and we didn't want to get lost here. With the wind blowing nearly straight into my face and the backpack weighing me down, I repeated my mantra over and over, "step by step," as we went up one hill and down the next.

An hour after eating my granola bar, my stomach was rumbling again and my pace was slowing. I was ready for lunch, but how could we stop in such weather?

"Don't worry," John said. "We'll find a place out of the wind and eat our sandwiches. There are natural caves in this area."

I saw some caves on the other side of the *wadi*, but because we still had a long way to go, I didn't want to walk far off our trail.

My mind wandered ahead. I knew that if we didn't get far enough along today, we would never make it to Sde Boker by tomorrow, and we had only two days' food and water.

We noticed a side *wadi* that looked promising. It appeared narrow enough to give some shelter and perhaps we'd find a cave there. But when our grotto never materialized, we settled on a relatively flat place between some boulders. Cheese sandwiches, an apple, an orange, and water had never tasted as good at home as they did in the open air after hiking five hours. We allowed ourselves one more energy bar for a treat. A light drizzle continued to fall intermittently.

"This is the kind of day for sitting in front of the stove with a good book and cup of hot cider," I said laughing, "and look at us!"

Soon we were on our feet and going again. Every small increment in elevation was a struggle. When it seemed we'd reached the highest ridge, there was another one in front of us. We were plodding across a long high plateau, leaning forward into the wind and steadying ourselves with our walking poles.

"Good thing we have backpacks," John said. On some stretches of the trail we had spoken a lot, but today we mostly concentrated on keeping going. "They keep us from being blown away."

I had looked at the map during lunch, and noticed that the next landmark was something called "fissures." And after that was "Gavei Hava," a natural rock formation.

"Do you think this could be them?" I asked.

"These are definitely the fissures," John said. "Look how deep they go!"

Now we knew that we weren't far from Gavei Hava. A *gev* in Hebrew is a low place where water collects after it rains, usually under a precipice.

Another twenty minutes on the desolate ridge and suddenly we came to a cleft in the ground. The trail signs pointed downward, which led us out of the wind, to our relief.

As we went steadily downward, the gap varied in width and at some points it was so steep that iron handholds were fastened into the rocks for the use of hikers.

"Throw your poles down to me. Turn around and come down backwards," John directed me. "Put your right foot on the iron, and I'll guide your left foot to this little rock step."

"I guess I wasn't paying enough attention to the map," I said. "I didn't notice that we had such a long steep descent."

"Uh huh, what goes up must come down." This was one of John's favorite expressions.

I pointed out that the Hebrew expression, "going down for the purpose of going up," fit better. In Israel, especially in the army, this is used to mean that something good will come out of a setback.

I was uneasy, realizing that we would eventually have to climb back out.

A half hour later the trail leveled out and we reached pools of water under a dry waterfall. We were in a deep canyon whose steep walls rose eighty meters above us. Covering the *wadi* floor were huge boulders, looking as if they had been tumbled over the sides by giants playing with stones up on top. The trail signs guided us over, under, and around the rocks in the narrow canyon. Stepping across gaps, lowering ourselves down, and pulling ourselves up, we slowly continued our descent along the valley floor. The drizzle turned into rain and fell progressively harder.

I began gazing up at the canyon walls and trying to figure out an escape route if the rain came in earnest. We had lived in Eilat in the south of Israel for thirty years and had made innumerable hikes in the Negev and Sinai Deserts, so I knew that one of the first rules for hiking in the winter is not to walk in the rain. I'm one of those people who like to read the small print on the back of maps, and there under *Instructions for Hikers* was written: "Before going out in winter, check with one of the Field Study Centers in the region, or with the meteorological service regarding flood warnings. Flash floods in the desert can be sudden and unexpected. During cloudy or rainy days, do not walk in *wadi* beds."

Not only had I read the small print, but I'd seen the force of flash floods with my own eyes. Years ago, when we lived in the Sinai on the Red Sea coast, we were camping on the beach and unbeknownst to us, it was raining up in the mountains. Suddenly, in the middle of the night, we heard a noise like a powerful generator, and the next thing we knew a wall of water was advancing down the *wadi*. We, as well as most of the other campers, instantly packed up our things and headed for higher ground. In the morning when it was light enough to see, a strange sight greeted us. A couple of modern day chariots were stuck in the waters of the Red Sea. The flood waters had washed several cars and a truck out to sea. It was the talk of the beach and a comical sight—to everyone except the vehicles' owners, who were sorry they hadn't bothered getting out of their sleeping bags to move their vehicles. The whole area where we had been staying was muddy and filled with boulders that had washed down with the water, and the smell of dampness filled the air.

Remembering that flash flood, I now thought, *What are we doing here? Are we crazy? We of all people should know not to be hiking on a day like this."* Alone in the *wadi*, surrounded by huge blocks of overturned stones, sheer rock faces on both sides, and the black sky far above us, all we could do was to keep moving along the trail. Should we have turned back when it began drizzling two hours outside Mitzpe Ramon? We had taken a risk, but we had felt the weather was likely to clear up. Or should we have stayed on the ridge and not descended the cleft into the canyon? At the time we'd been protected from the forceful, biting wind; we hadn't stopped to consider the danger of being in a *wadi* if the rain intensified.

*No one even knows where we are.* We had entered another universe and were its only inhabitants.

"God, please get us out of here alive," I prayed.

Thirty-two years ago, in an oasis in the Sinai, I had begun reading the Bible, and God had completely changed my life. Since then, prayer has been a regular aspect of my life. At home, however, prayer was usually relegated to regular times in the day: after getting up in the morning, before meals, at bedtime. Now on the Israel Trail, we had been getting into the habit of talking to

God as we strode along—praying for friends as they came to mind and involving Him in our decisions.

When we came to a giant mushroom-shaped rock, John suggested that we rest for a few minutes. Crouching below the overhang I felt as if we were two dwarfs under their toadstool taking shelter from the rain.

It felt good to stop and catch our breath in a dry place and to be on slightly higher ground. In fact, I felt so safe and comfortable that I proposed we stay there for the night. It wasn't exactly as flat as we would like for a sleeping spot, nor was it much bigger than the area of our two sleeping bags, but we'd probably be safe from the flood waters.

John, however, insisted that we keep going. It was only 2:30 P.M., too early to stop for the night. I knew he was right and so had no choice but to hoist my backpack onto my shoulders and continue. Thankfully the rain was tapering off. The *wadi* was getting narrower—a sign that we were coming to the end—when we noticed a Trail sign pointing up the cliff face on the left.

"Thank you, God; we're going to get out of this place," I murmured.

Soon we were scrambling hands and feet up the side of the canyon, following the white, blue and orange signs. The trail was vertical and I was getting tired, but at least I knew that we wouldn't be washed away by a flood.

To our shock we came to a place that looked nearly impassable. We either had to step out on a narrow ledge that dropped off steeply on one side while hugging the rock wall on the other side, or take off our packs and crawl under a lengthy, low overhang. There was no other way around. I wasn't ready for this; I thought we had passed the danger zone. If I had been thirty years younger, I might have relished the challenge; but today I shudder when I remember some of the crazy things I used to do for fun, such as parachuting out of an airplane or fording a raging glacial river.

I couldn't believe that the Trails Authority didn't put iron handholds in this spot. What did they expect from us? It was apparent to me that this trail was made for folks who had just finished the army in a Special Forces unit. At fifty-four years old I could do very well without the adrenaline rush, thank you.

We chose what looked like the safer of the two options. "No big deal," said John. "I'll crawl through first and check it out."

Though he tried not to show it, I could sense that even John was tense. The rocks were wet and slick from the rain. I watched anxiously, my heart pounding in my chest, as John disappeared around the corner and out of sight.

"I made it! No problem," he yelled back.

John crept back to me and then went through a second time dragging his pack behind him, no easy task over the rough ground. I heard the rocks crunching under his knees and then thump! A water bottle fell and rolled down the hill. It stopped a few meters below us on a rocky crag, before tumbling into thin air.

"Never mind," John said. "We've got too much water with us anyway. Less weight to carry."

John passed through a third time slowly pulling my pack. Then it was my turn. If John could do it with the packs, I could do it without them.

"Just look straight ahead," I told myself. "Don't look down." I inched my way along the length of the ledge, somehow maneuvering our four walking sticks in one hand. I discovered on this trip that I didn't like edges and ledges.

When we eventually reached the top of the hill, we followed the trail along the canyon's rim.

"Be careful on these slippery rocks," John warned. I shuffled my feet along, keeping my eyes on the trail.

"Wow, look at those caves," said John. Across the canyon we could see caves that were obviously man-made. "Monks probably lived in them."

We were close to the ruins of ancient Avdat, a city founded by the Nabateans as a major station along the Spice Route from Arabia to Gaza in the third century B.C. Although history surrounds us in Israel and remnants of bygone civilizations are everywhere, we didn't expect to encounter any ruins out here in the middle of the wilderness. Sites excavated by the Antiquities Department are marked on maps; however, with the wealth of history in Israel, many sites either haven't been investigated or are considered too insignificant to warrant a map notation.

The Romans conquered Avdat in A.D. 106. Later, during the Byzantine Empire, the city experienced its peak of prosperity, and many Nabateans converted to Christianity. Hundreds of caves are scattered around the area that contain crosses etched into the stone walls and ceilings. John was certain that these caves were used by monks. Only later, after checking the Internet at home, did I discover that John's guess was correct.

The Nabatean civilization always fascinated us, so we were excited to discover these caves in an isolated *wadi*. Visiting preserved archaeological sites is interesting, but stumbling upon a place unexpectedly brings a special thrill. We would have been happy to sleep in one of the caves, but they were unfortunately on the other side of the wide canyon. Furthermore, the resident monks must have preferred total peace and quiet, because the only way they could have entered was by being lowered in a basket. We began looking for a more accessible cave.

According to our map we would soon be coming out of our *wadi*, Nahal Hava, into a broad valley. (*Nahal* is the Hebrew word for a stream that is dry in the summer.) That didn't suit us at all. We would be exposed again to the wind and the rain, and in danger of being swept away by floods if the rain intensified. It was getting late; we were tired, and we needed to find a place to camp, preferably in a cave.

It's not always easy to find the right cave with a smooth

flat floor, a high enough ceiling, and not too far off the path.
Finally, up a side *wadi*, we spotted what looked like a possibility.
We walked up the streambed for about ten minutes, jumping
across pools of water that had already formed from the rain. John
clambered up to the cave to check it out.

"Looks okay to me. Come on up and see what you think. Grab
some sticks of wood on your way."

The floor of the cave was covered in a thick layer of animal
dung. We weren't sure from what—bats, doves, ibexes? John
bravely walked to the end, and produced an old bone. Did that
mean this was also home to carnivores such as foxes and hyenas?

"It's warm in here," he said, "and if we put up our tent, we'll
be really cozy."

Piling some sticks together at the cave's entrance, John started
a campfire to cook our evening meal and to warm us. Soon we
were coughing and choking from the smoke.

With my eyes stinging and watering, I couldn't see to get
the pot and food out of my pack. "Cave men must have done it
differently," I said. We obviously had to move the fire out to a
rock shelf below our cave. I could only hope that the cave would
be smoke-free by the time we wanted to sleep.

"I didn't realize all the smoke would go straight inside,"
admitted John. "At least we must have smoked out any animals."
We still had lessons to learn about camping. Little did we realize
at the time how many. Later on our trip we stayed with a friend
who is an archaeologist. When we enthusiastically told him stories
about the Israel Trail, including our night in the cave, he informed
us that we had placed ourselves in a dangerous situation.

"You could have contracted 'cave fever'," he said, telling us
that many archaeologists have been infected.

Cave fever, also known as "relapsing fever," is found in the
dust of ten percent of caves in Israel. A parasite in the bite
of contaminated soft ticks transmits the disease. These miniature

blood-suckers take brief meals lasting less than half an hour, usually at night. The bite is painless, and the unfortunate victim is unaware of his plight until he begins to suffer from weakness, joint and muscle pain, and headaches. Paralysis as well as neurological, kidney, liver, and blood damage follow, unless the sufferer is treated with antibiotics. The bite is sometimes lethal.

At the time we weren't aware of potential hazards lurking in our cave. We simply sought shelter. Sleeping in our tent may have protected us from the ticks.

The smoke eventually cleared out; we finished our meal and stretched out in our sleeping bags, falling asleep to the sound of pattering rain.

"Are you happy?" I asked.

"Uh huh," answered John. "D'you realize we didn't meet another person all day?"

"Who would venture out in this weather?"

---

1. The word "jeep" in this account is used generically for a small, durable, general-purpose four-wheel drive vehicle like those used by the U.S. Army during and after World War II, which gained popularity for civilian recreation and scientific explorations. One manufacturer has capitalized and trademarked the word.

# 2. Birth of a Dream

For the past twenty years, our life has revolved around managing the Shelter Hostel. A hostel is like a fire station—it's open 24/7, 365 days a year. In order to keep our sanity, we need a break once in a while. For us, a trip into the desert is the best way to rest and revive. Long before we ever dreamed of the Israel Trail, we were accustomed to taking quick jaunts of a day or two into the wilderness.

"What d'you think about the Sinai?" John suggested one winter day. "It's been a few years since we gave it a try. Maybe they've crossed my name off their black list by now."

During the time we lived in the Sinai, the ruling Egyptians discouraged contact between outsiders and the local Bedouin residents. Our friendships with the Bedouins, as well as the Bibles and cassette tapes we gave them, resulted in John's becoming persona non grata in Egypt.

I could already picture myself leaning back in a palm-thatched hut on a quiet beach and snorkeling among the multi-colored fish and coral. And I liked the idea that, from our home in Eilat, we could be there in an hour after crossing the border.

The Sinai held a special attraction for me. Having grown up outside Washington, D.C., I traveled to Alaska with a friend during the summer vacation after my first year of college. I wanted to get away from modern civilization, and I ended up in one of the most isolated places in the United States. In a small Eskimo village above the Arctic Circle I learned to hunt and to fish and to appreciate such delicacies as bear ribs, caribou heart, seal blubber, and ptarmigan wings. After three years in Alaska, however, I had the urge to see the rest of the world and flew to Europe, with the hope of continuing on to India. Before undertaking the long overland journey east, I decided to stop in Israel.

Although I was brought up in a Jewish home, my family was not religious and I became more interested in Eastern philosophies than in the faith of my fathers. After arriving at Ben Gurion Airport, I spent three months on the farm of my Israeli relatives, and then decided to travel south to the Sinai, part of Israel then. Most people wouldn't immediately see a resemblance between Alaska and the Sinai Desert, but the wide expanses of the Sinai and its sparse population reminded me of the Arctic that I loved. Bedouins, like Eskimos, lived close to nature.

Bedouin, meaning "desert dweller," refers to nomadic Arab groups in the Sahara, Sinai, Negev, and Arabian Deserts. The term evokes images of black tents, veiled women, men in long flowing robes, thick aromatic coffee, and camel caravans. Until the middle of the last century, nearly all Bedouins lived a traditional existence—divided into tribes, each led by a Sheikh herding camels, sheep, and goats, and riding their highly-prized horses.

The Bedouin lifestyle was shaped by the desert environment. Since few places in this barren region are able to sustain even a small population for an extended period of time, they were forced to be ever on the move, migrating from oasis to oasis with their herds.

Such extreme conditions shaped their character also, and Bedouins are renowned for their tribal loyalty, fierceness to outsiders, hospitality to guests, and generosity. In recent years the grazing ranges have shrunk while the population has multiplied. Israel's small land area and the overall process of modernization has led to more contact between the Bedouin and the other Israelis. The influence of the outside world has aroused, particularly in the young people, a desire for improved standards of living. Thus most Bedouins today live and work in or near cities.

Similar to all people groups in transition, many Bedouins have yet to find their place in the modern society. A generation gap has developed between the elders and the young people, and the newcomers from the countryside are looked down upon by their urban neighbors.

Living with Bedouins, I learned to eat rice and goat stew mixed with the coarse black hairs of the goats, to savor curdled goat's milk churned in a skin, and to sift worms out of flour before we made bread. I ended up in Nueiba, a Bedouin village on the Red Sea, which also included an Israeli agricultural settlement, and travelers like me who slept on the beach. The transparent blue waters, graceful palm trees, and white sand dunes enticed me to stay longer.

Being in Israel awoke in me a desire to know more about the history of this land. The Bible, I decided, would be a good place to begin, since I realized that I knew almost nothing about it. In Jerusalem someone had given me a Bible and in Nueiba, with plenty of time on my hands, I started to read. Slowly I began to believe what I was reading, and a new world opened up before me. I had done a lot of stupid things and felt unable to break free from bad relationships and bad habits.

In the Bible, I encountered a God who cared about me, loved me, and offered me the chance to set the past behind me and to start over. I discovered that it's possible to have a personal relationship with God. My life was transformed.

My family expected that I would deepen my Jewish roots in Israel. I did so in a way that no one would have expected; I started to believe in Jesus, and felt more Jewish than ever. I discovered the inner peace I had been searching for. Later I met John in Jerusalem and found that he, coming from Holland, had had a similar spiritual experience. Nine months after we met each other we were married in the U.S., with my parents as our witnesses, and our housekeeper as the only other guest.

After our wedding we settled in Key West, Florida for a year before immigrating to Israel, where for several years we lived in a tent in the Sinai. When the Sinai was given back to Egypt in 1982, we moved to Eilat but we continued to visit our Bedouin friends.

On one of our trips we discovered that the Egyptian secret police were looking for John because of our close association with the Bedouins and the Bibles we gave them. The next time we tried to enter Egypt, we were turned back at the border.

This time, as we planned a short trip to the Sinai, we decided we would be prepared for either being admitted or refused entry. Tossing a change of clothes, our bathing suits, snorkels, and camera into our bags, we were on our way to the Taba border, fifteen minutes from our home. At first it looked as if things were going smoothly. We produced our passports, and the border guard typed our names into his computer.

"Oh no," John whispered. "They've become computerized. This doesn't look good." In the old days they sometimes didn't bother to look in their books, especially if there was a long line.

The guard handed me back my stamped passport and was about to stamp John's when he hesitated.

"Sorry. Cannot go to Egypt," he said.

"Why not?" John asked, unwilling to take 'no' for an answer.

The guard shrugged his shoulders.

"He barely speaks English," I said to John. "There's no point in arguing. You won't get an answer from him." My dreams of long beach walks and snorkeling popped like a balloon landing on a thorn tree.

What should we do now? We crossed back into Israel and sat on the beach near the border to think. Go to Jerusalem or to Jordan, or visit one of our children up north? No place but the Sinai attracted us, but we also didn't want to go home.

Running a hostel in Eilat was more than a job for us; it was a way of life and a ministry. Once the children were born, we couldn't travel as we used to, but the hostel kept us in touch with people from all over the world.

The Shelter, as we call it, affords us many opportunities to help people—providing for their physical needs, guiding people on their spiritual journey, aiding battered women, drug addicts and alcoholics, and dealing with the special needs of new immigrants and foreign workers. Our forty beds were full nearly all year long, with guests staying anywhere from one night to a couple of years. Most visitors paid for their lodging, but those who couldn't were able to help with cleaning, gardening, painting, or other jobs, in exchange for room and board. We couldn't imagine any other life, but occasionally we needed to get away, and we had prepared our staff to manage without us for three days.

We didn't want to spend our precious vacation time sitting on the beach debating what to do; so we decided to get in our jeep and start driving. If not the Sinai, why not the Negev Desert?

The desert has a special place in our hearts. I sometimes ask myself if it's because we have lived for thirty years in Eilat, a town surrounded by desert, and familiarity with any natural environment would have the same effect. Or is there something intrinsic in the desert itself that speaks to us? The stark, empty, and expansive landscape provides long vistas and jagged edges. There are few living things. Your eyes catch the slightest movement of a bird, a camel, or an ibex, however far in the distance. The utter silence is broken only by the sound of the wind and of the persistent flies. Even a short day trip into the desert requires knowledge and careful planning in order to survive.

In contrast, I grew up hiking in the Appalachian Mountain forests of the American East Coast. Dense and teeming with life, the forest is different from the desert. It envelopes and confines you, and you don't know what it may be hiding. A person or an animal could sneak up on you with no warning. The richness of forest life fills your senses with scents of flowers, mosses, and rotting wood, and with sounds of bird songs, animal noises, and rushing water.

Then why do I love the desert? The Hebrew word for desert is *midbar*, which is usually translated in the Bible as "wilderness." *Midbar* has many meanings, among them: an uninhabited land, uncultivated, and without vegetation. In short, the opposite of what makes life convenient and comfortable, the antithesis of civilization. In Hebrew every word has a three-letter root and the same root for *midbar* is found in *daber* which means "to speak." What is the connection? The desert is void of distractions. When all our props are removed and life gets down to the basics, words come through clearly and loudly. Certainly many great men of the Bible heard from God in the desert. Abraham, Moses, Elijah, David, John the Baptist, Jesus, Paul, and others—all encountered God and experienced spiritual renewal in the wilderness.

So the desert it would be. Feeling the need of renewal ourselves, and having decided on a jeep trip to the Negev, it didn't take us long to prepare. We loaded water, food, bedding, and extra gas into the jeep and were soon on our way north. An hour out of Eilat we left the paved highway and civilization behind. Slowly we entered into the rhythm of the desert, and it had its usual effect—quieting, allowing us to forget for a time the things that normally clamor for our attention.

Finally, after a day and a half of bumping along remote jeep trails, sleeping under the stars, climbing mountains, and not seeing

another person, we were about two hours away from the outlying
settlement of Kadesh Barnea where we had some friends. Suddenly
we noticed an army jeep on a hill in the distance, driving in our
direction.

"This doesn't look good," John remarked.

The jeep came to a halt directly in front of us and an officer
stepped out. "What are you doing here? Do you know where you
are?" he questioned us.

"Right here," I said, pointing to our map.

"Yes, but this is a closed military area."

"We didn't see any signs," John protested.

"The local Bedouins take them down," he said. "Follow me."

We followed his jeep in the opposite direction than we had
planned to go. He left us when we reached his base, and he pointed
us in the direction of the road.

*What are we doing back on the highway?* I thought. Spontane-
ity isn't one of my strong points, and I couldn't believe that our
plans were being thwarted a second time.

John decided that since it was getting late, we should drive
to Sde Boker, a nearby settlement, or *kibbutz*, and duck into the
*wadi* behind it. Trying not to be discouraged, I bounced along
next to John in the jeep, map in hand, searching for a camping
spot. The total darkness of the desert surrounded us by the time
we stopped outside of the Ein Zik Nature Reserve. (*Ein* means
"spring" in Hebrew.)

In the flickering light of our campfire, John shared with me
his conviction that God was trying to tell us something. I had to
agree, as I realized that twice now our plans had been changed
drastically, and here we were in a place we had never even heard
of before.

We lay on our backs looking up at the millions of stars in the
cloudless black sky. This is what I'd been longing for—the stillness
of the desert, the simple life. John reminded me that the children

of Israel, after they left Egypt, were on their way to the Promised
Land, and could have soon reached it, when God turned them back
at Kadesh Barnea. We had been getting close to Kadesh Barnea
ourselves this afternoon when we were turned back.

"But weren't they stopped because of disobedience?" I asked.

John explained that Moses and the children of Israel arrived
in Kadesh Barnea after an eleven-day journey from Mt. Horeb,
or Sinai. From here Moses sent out twelve spies to explore the
land. Ten brought back a negative report and only two, Joshua
and Caleb, encouraged the people to trust in God to fulfill His
promises. Israel could have gone directly into Canaan, but instead
God determined that they would wander in the desert for forty
years. They spent most of that time in the area of Kadesh Barnea.

"I'm not saying that God is punishing us for disobedience, that
that's the reason we couldn't get into the Sinai or drive to Kadesh,
but I still think He's trying to show us something," John said.

"Yes, the way everything happened these past two days, and
then we end up here," I said. "Tomorrow in the light we'll see what
kind of place this is." After a moment I added, "The soldiers in the
jeep were actually pretty nice. It wasn't really their fault."

We were soon in our sleeping bags.

"Do you see that satellite? And hey, there's a shooting star."
Since I was little, I've been fascinated by astronomy.

"*Lila tov* (Good night)," John said. "I love you."

We woke at dawn and were stunned to see what a beautiful place
we had landed in. Brown hills and a sparkling blue sky provided a
vivid backdrop to abundant spiky green palms.

"Wow, this place is amazing! You know, it reminds me of
Elim from the Bible, where Moses camped with the children of
Israel," John said eagerly. "It was a place of twelve springs and
seventy palm trees."

"Could this be it?"

"Nah. Elim was in the south Sinai close to where Moses and the children of Israel crossed the Red Sea."

Ein Zik seemed to us a classic and dreamy picture of a desert oasis. In the fresh air of the early morning we walked among the palm trees, looking for a comfortable spot to sit and read our Bibles. Rounding a bend, we chanced upon a small tent on the path and two young people emerging.

"Shalom! How did you get here?" John asked. "I didn't see any jeep. My name's John, and this is my wife, Judy."

"I'm Uri," the young man introduced himself. "We entered Ein Zik from the south, came down that cliff back there. We left Eilat eighteen days ago on the Israel Trail."

We were impressed. Hiking straight for eighteen days? With all their possessions on their backs?

Not wishing to disturb them, however, as it looked as if they had just awakened, we walked on. We sat down side by side on a rocky projection overlooking the oasis, but had trouble concentrating on what we were reading.

After a few minutes John began, "I've got an idea."

"I know what it is." We'd been married twenty-eight years, after all.

"We'll walk the Israel Trail," he continued.

"That's what I was thinking."

We turned back to our Bibles and tried to read.

"Let's do it before my sixtieth birthday." That was in two years.

"We'll have to find someone to take care of the hostel."

"And the congregation too."

"Let's call our walk, 'Arise, Walk the Land'." That's a well-known Israeli folk song, taken from a verse in Genesis.

"We could make tracts to give out to people we meet on the way."

"We'll invite our kids and other people to walk with us."

"But mostly we want to do it alone."

"Sure."

"We can stay with friends along the way."

"How about T-shirts?"

"Wonder if those kids are still there."

"I'll keep a diary."

The couple was just rolling up their tent when we got back, and they were more than happy to talk. We found out that they were from a *kibbutz* in the north and knew a friend of our daughter's. Now we tried to ask all the questions we could think of about the Israel Trail.

"We carry water for three days at the most," they explained. Securing water is one of the chief concerns of anyone traveling in the desert. They went on to say that they were taking it slowly. They hadn't spent time training, but were getting into shape as they went along. They offered to let us try their packs on so that we could feel how much weight they were carrying. That was another big concern: the backpacks. We enjoy hiking, but not with forty kilos on our backs.

"They never weigh more than twenty-five kilos," they added helpfully. These kids were young. Could *we* handle it? I was used to hiking with one water bottle and my camera.

They looked happy, however, and eager to begin their day's walk. Besides, there was something intriguing about the Israel Trail. It reminded us of other well-known trails in the world—the Appalachian Trail, the Camino de Santiago in Spain, the Milford Track in New Zealand. We had heard about the existence of an Israel Trail but had never before met anyone who had walked it.

As we left Ein Zik and drove back down Nahal Sin, the desert landscape dazzled me with its many shades of brown and seemingly endless ranges of hills. I was already imagining myself on the Israel Trail. Could we really walk it in its entirety? Driving the whole length of Israel took about eight hours; how long would walking take? Maybe this was a crazy idea that would quickly pass. I began to wish I had asked Uri more questions. Were they sleeping out every night? What kind of food did they take? And clothes? How long did they expect the whole journey to take?

We were both in fairly good shape and liked to hike, but this was a huge jump from anything we had ever done before. When our four children were little, we used to go out with the babies on our backs and take short hikes, and as they grew older we ventured farther. Now, with Josh, Racheli, Moriah and Yonatan grown up, we enjoyed the challenge of setting out with a map to discover new places. But we never went for longer than a day.

We had been feeling the need for a break lately. We heard of people who took sabbaticals. Going back to school with a bunch of twenty-year-olds, sitting around in a little cabin, studying all day in a dark library, sailing across the ocean—none of these things appealed to us. So perhaps walking the Israel Trail would suit us; it was a chance to be out in nature and to become more deeply acquainted with the land of Israel. Walking twenty-five kilometers (or 15.5 miles) a day might just give us the perfect chance to relax. Uri and his girlfriend seemed to be the kind of people we could relate to. Unlike many young people that we find in cities these days who are looking for action and for nightlife, they cared for the outdoors and for spiritual things. If these were the type of folks we would meet on the Trail, then that was another reason to hike it.

After a couple of hours we were back on the highway to Eilat and our mobile phone had reception again. John began dialing.

"Hey, we're out of the desert. Things worked out differently than we thought. We never made it to the Sinai or to Kadesh Barnea, but ended up in Ein Zik. But guess what? We've decided to do the Israel Trail."

I cringed. Why did he have to tell everyone already? We didn't know what would come of our idea. It seemed to me that there were an awful lot of obstacles in the way of our making the hike.

"I'm not telling everyone. That was just Josh, Racheli, Moriah and Yonatan. But okay, we'll just tell the kids. And start praying about it."

# 3. A Taste of the Trail

When we came home from our jeep trip John's birthday was approaching, and I could think of only one present I wanted to buy him. I went to our local bookstore and asked for a book about the Israel Trail. I was delighted to find just what I was looking for: *Shvil Israel* in Hebrew, or *Israel Trail* in English, by Tzvi Gilat, a colorful illustrated guide with lots of maps. (*Shvil* means "path" in Hebrew.)

John loved his present. He glanced through it with appreciation that I hadn't given up on our vision, but was taking a step, albeit a small one, to make our dream become a reality.

I, however, read the book from cover to cover and studied the maps till I could practically recite the route of the Trail by heart. I learned that, after fifteen years of planning and work, the Israel National Trail was dedicated in 1995. Although thousands of kilometers of marked hiking trails already existed, the goal of the *Shvil* was to serve as a backbone connecting some of the choicest among them.

The Israel Trail traverses 940 kilometers (about 600 miles) of mountains and valleys from Israel's northernmost point at the Lebanese border to its southern tip at the Red Sea, nearly twice the length of Israel. And unlike the Appalachian Trail, for instance, the Israel Trail also winds its way through inhabited areas: along the edges of *kibbutzim* and *moshavim*, through Arab towns and villages, and even through Tel Aviv, Israel's largest city. It passes along Jewish, Christian, Moslem and Druze holy sites. The book soon occupied an esteemed place on our living room coffee table.

Our life is busy. In addition to managing the Shelter Hostel, John is the leader of the Eilat Congregation, a group of people from many different countries—Israeli Jews and Arabs, North and South Americans, Europeans and Russians, Africans and many others—joined together because we all believe that Jesus is the Messiah.

We gather together as a spiritual family on Saturdays, the day of rest in Israel, and throughout the week have meetings in homes for the Spanish, Hebrew, Russian, and English speakers. People fill our lives from morning till night. So after coming home from our jeep trip we didn't have a lot of time to sit around and think about the Israel Trail. Occasionally, however, the subject would come up, and we began to talk about the logistics of the trip.

Several friends, our age or younger, had developed health problems: a knee ache, back pain, cancer. "I don't think we should wait till you're sixty," I said to John. Our current good health might continue for years, but there was no guarantee. "It seems to me that the sooner we do the Trail, the better."

"Yeah, you're right," John agreed. "We're not getting any younger. But there's still the problem of who could take over the hostel and the congregation while we're gone." According to our calculations, we needed about two months to complete the journey.

"Which season should we do it in?" I asked.

"Obviously either spring or fall." Israel has a Mediterranean climate defined by two seasons: the wet winter from October through March, and the long dry summer. Furthermore, for a small country, only 470 kilometers from Metulla in the north to Eilat in the south, there are enormous differences in weather and geography. Jerusalem receives the same yearly rainfall as London—approximately 670 millimeters (26 inches). While London's rainfall is spread throughout the year, though, Jerusalem's is condensed into five or six months. So, for half the year in Jerusalem it's important to have an umbrella handy. In Eilat, an umbrella is completely unnecessary, since it usually rains only five times a year—a mere thirty millimeters (1.2 inches) total. In Beer Sheva, three hours north of Eilat, it rains six times that much.

The temperatures also vary tremendously throughout the land. A typical winter day in Jerusalem is a brisk 5°C (41°F), while on that same day people may be sunbathing in Eilat. Summers, on the other hand, are brutal in Eilat, with daily temperatures over 40°C (104°F), whereas in Jerusalem, 800 meters above sea level, it remains a comfortable 20°C (68°F). All this had to be taken into account as we planned the time of our trip.

Months passed and winter turned into spring and then into summer. I couldn't push the idea of the Israel National Trail out of my mind. In quiet moments my thoughts drifted to the *Shvil* and I enjoyed flipping through the book by Tzvi Gilat. I especially liked the picture of the author on the last page when he had reached the end of his journey and was waving his hand at the photographer with the Red Sea in the background. I could just picture myself, having trekked through the whole land, finally arriving home to a cheering group of friends and family, tired but happy.

The book often made its way to my bedside table. I dreamed and prayed, while all the time trying not to become too attached to our plan. I asked myself how I would feel if things didn't work out. Would I be disappointed? Not too much, I hoped. After all, we had laid it in God's hands and asked for His guidance; He could open or close doors.

Our lives are far from boring. We have hosted guests from

more than eighty countries in our hostel. We have witnessed lives changed from darkness to light, from addiction to freedom, from dysfunction to wholeness. We have traveled to Mongolia and Malaysia, Indonesia and Ethiopia. But the notion of hiking the Israel Trail gripped me as no trip had ever done before.

During winter we hike several times a month in the hills around Eilat, a small city of 50,000 people sandwiched between rough brown mountains and the sparkling waters of the Red Sea. But by May, when we feel like collapsing after thirty minutes in the punishing heat, our walking is put on hold until the cooler weather returns in late October. The winter before we hiked the Israel Trail, several providential encounters with the Trail occurred, though we weren't even looking for them.

One time, on our way home from a trip to northern Israel, we decided we had time to stop and hike for a couple of hours. We saw a Nature Reserve sign that read *Pura Reserve*. Having driven by this park many times without entering it, we were now curious; and we eagerly turned off the road.

The landscape featured low rolling hills covered with dry grasses and wheat fields, typical of the northern Negev Desert. The path, meandering along an old broken-down Turkish railway bridge, was a pleasant break from our long car journey.

"Jupe, look!" exclaimed John. "Here it is, the Israel Trail!"

Sure enough, the white, blue, and orange-striped trail sign was clearly visible on the rocks. We followed it for several kilometers, pausing in a grove of eucalyptus trees.

As I looked around and admired the majestic old trees and the smooth ground underneath, I could envision us camping here while on the Trail. Our dream began to take on a new life; we had tasted a tiny morsel of the *Shvil*.

Another time that winter, we visited our youngest son, Yonatan, at the Herzliya marina on the Mediterranean Sea. His compulsory military service was in the navy, and that week his patrol boat was guarding the central coast. It was the kind of day that invited a walk on the beach. I relished the sea wind blowing in my hair, the waves crashing on the beach, and the small white clouds floating high in the sky.

"Hey, look! I can't believe it!" shouted John. "There's an Israel Trail sign. Did you know that the Trail goes right along the beach here?"

"I was trying to figure out what it did in this area," I replied. "According to the Trail Book, it passes east of Tel Aviv and only hits the beach up near Caesarea. But our road atlas shows the Trail following this whole stretch of coast. Could there be alternate routes?"

"It seems that we're finding the Trail all over the place." John's enthusiasm was growing also.

His resolve not to tell anyone about our dream didn't last. Before long he was telling everyone, and I stopped cringing. Our children were even telling their friends about their parents' plan to walk the Israel Trail. Occasionally one of them would call and say, "Hey, Mom! There's this guy studying with me who walked the *Shvil* last year." Or, "I got a ride with some guys who just finished the Trail." We noticed that most of the hikers were closer to college age than to retirement age like us.

The major problem was still finding someone to take care of the Shelter and the congregation while we were gone. But John's broadcasting our plans to everyone ended up working to our advantage. Our friend, Jim, came to visit us from California and as usual John started off by saying, "Judy and I plan on walking the Israel Trail. ... What? Never heard of it? ... It goes from Eilat to Dan, 850 kilometers. The idea came to us last winter when we were out in our jeep. 'Arise, walk the land' we call our trip."

When Jim asked how we would manage the Shelter and congregation in our absence, John conceded it was a bit of a problem, but he knew something would work out. We were praying and waiting for someone to come along who could take over the ministry.

"How long will this walk take?" asked Jim.

"We figure about two months," John answered.

"How about if I were to come?" Jim offered. "I could stay for four or five weeks. When do you want to go?"

I could hardly believe what I was hearing. Was Jim the answer to our prayers? We could surely find someone to fill in the extra weeks. I was scared to believe it was true.

"When do you want to go?" Jim asked.

"Ideally we'd like to walk it in the spring," I replied. "Before it gets too hot and while we can enjoy the flowers."

Now we could attach a date onto our plan. The main barrier had been cleared for our dream to become reality.


The days were becoming shorter and cooler. Autumn was filled with holidays—Rosh Hashanah, Yom Kippur, and the Feast of Tabernacles. Even more than the usual stream of visitors flooded our lives—visitors, people, and more people. We seemed to have no time for ourselves.

At my usual gym classes I reminded myself that I was preparing for the Israel Trail. Stomach crunches and leg lifts, exercise bands and hand weights, Pilates and aerobics were all sweated out in anticipation of our journey. But I felt it wasn't enough.

"It's about time we started getting in shape for our walk," I declared to John, "if it's really going to happen in February." Although we had been exceptionally busy, it was already November and we hadn't started training yet.

"All right," agreed John. "Tomorrow I'll take off and we'll try to get out every week from now on."

I wanted to start with a serious hike and then the next time to try one with backpacks.

We looked at our maps and chose the area around Nahal Barak, a deep canyon. After driving for an hour, we stepped out of the jeep and realized we had forgotten our map.

Going into the desert without a map isn't smart. In fact, I had come to equate using a map as our guide on hikes to using the Bible as my guide through life; I try not to go very far without either of them. Through experience I've discovered that in places where trails cross, where the terrain isn't familiar, or where there are many obstacles, it's particularly important to refer often to either the map or to the Bible.

Instead of trying to determine whose fault it was and accusing each other, we just started walking because the area was familiar to us. I knew that many things could go wrong in our upcoming Israel Trail hike and that we would have to pull together as a couple. It seemed as good a time as any to practice teamwork, and it was both exhilarating and healing to be out in the desert we loved.

We did well climbing up through the deep gorge and onto the hill behind it. My mind kept running ahead and thinking about what food to bring, what it would be like to sleep out every night, and what equipment we needed to buy. From the top we had a view of the Arava Valley and the mountains of Edom. The Arava is part of the Rift Valley between Israel and Jordan.

John, who never liked returning the same way he had come, remembered from the map that we could hike down one of the little *wadi*s, and that eventually we would connect with the main trail.

"Which one did we take the last time, Jupe? Don't you remember?"

I found it impossible to say because they all looked the same. In any case, I don't like leaving the path, whereas John likes nothing better than bushwhacking. But in the interest of preparing for the Trail I didn't argue with him.

John charged down the *wadi*, scrambling over boulders.

"Whatcha think? Look familiar?" he asked.

We both have a good sense of direction and the territory wasn't strange to us, but down in a narrow gorge, it's hard to keep your bearings. After half an hour of steep descent we stood on top of an impassable *mapal*, a cliff that turns into a waterfall every couple of years when it rains hard enough. John examined our position from all angles, but finally even he had to conclude that there was no choice but to turn back. Up we climbed until we reached the same level from which we had descended.

I was pleased with myself for not saying, "I told you so." It was vital for both of us that this practice hike should succeed; it would be a foretaste of how we would manage on the Trail.

We hadn't eaten for five hours, but since there was no wood around, we couldn't even cook ourselves a little pita bread and a cup of tea as we usually did, so we dipped our cucumbers and tomatoes into the hummus and called that lunch.

"Look, Jupe." John pointed to a spot in the distance where we were supposed to finish. "We can still take a shortcut back to the Barak Canyon by cutting across that plain."

"Oh, come on. We already lost two hours on the last shortcut and if we make a wrong turn this time, we won't get back by dark," I insisted. "So this time, let's just stick to the marked trail we came on." John didn't argue.

The last part of the trail was a long steep drop. Normally I prefer going down hills rather than up, because it's easier on my heart and lungs, but this time my right knee began to hurt. At first I didn't want to tell John. It wasn't unbearable, and I hated to disappoint him. What would this mean for our plans? When I finally did mention it to John, he confessed that his left knee was also hurting, although from his description, not as badly as mine. The sun was going down when we arrived at our car, and when we stopped, the pain went away. However, it made me question whether I would be able to make the journey. I didn't want to succeed in walking the Israel Trail but cause permanent damage to my knee. I decided to make an appointment to see the orthopedist. Better to know as soon as possible the truth about my knee and if necessary to forget about the Trail. Would John want or be able to do it without me? I didn't think so.

When I came home I made a list of what I'd learned from our trek:

- *Don't forget the map.*
- *Carry snacks such as nuts and dried fruit in case we can't make a fire.*
- *Take it easy and have fun.*
- *Travel light.*

Two weeks later I entered the orthopedist's office, having decided that I would accept his diagnosis as a sign of whether or not we were meant to walk the *Shvil*.

As I lay on the examining table, he twisted my leg into all sorts of unnatural positions. "Does this hurt?" he asked. "This?"

He finally stopped and explained, "It's nothing serious, just a stretched ligament. Let's put it this way," he said smiling. "At our age, if you get up in the morning and nothing hurts at all, then you're dead. So don't worry, your trek won't damage your knee, and if you have any pain, just take ibuprofen." I made a mental note to add that to the list of first aid supplies we needed, and called John to announce that the trip was still on.

The month of December didn't allow much time to think about the Trail. At Christmas we celebrated the Shelter Hostel's twentieth anniversary and organized a big reunion with old Shelter friends, guests, and staff. Grocery shopping, preparing guest lists, menus, and a PowerPoint slide presentation, as well as coordinating the program, occupied all our attention. By the time the last guests had left, we had a month till Jim was due to arrive on February 4. We hadn't bought our equipment yet nor written the tract that we planned to take with us. On our hike we anticipated meeting many people, and we wanted a small pamphlet to introduce them to who we were, why we were walking the Trail, and what we believed, with an invitation to stay in the Shelter.

"I'd feel a lot better if we had our camping equipment and could start trying it out," I told John at breakfast one morning.

"Okay, where to?" John asked, grabbing his car keys. "I've got two hours before I have to be at the Shelter. Will that be long enough to buy everything?"

"Sure," I said, "I've checked it out. We need a tent and stove, sleeping bags, packs, sleeping pads, and about fifteen maps. Two stores in Eilat sell this kind of gear, but Yoni in the mall seemed the most helpful to me."

The store was busy, but in the half hour we waited for help, we looked over the various items on my list of necessary gear. The backpacks were certainly a lot different from the chunky square ones we had lugged around while wandering the world thirty years ago. Instead of external frames and outside pockets, these had internal frames; the packs were sleek and the prices steep. John took the cheapest one down from the wall, tried it on, and decided that it was for him.

Finally Yoni approached us. "I'd like to explain to you some of the principles involved in choosing a backpack," he began with a smile. "A pack is like a shoe—it has to fit exactly. What fits you might not fit someone else. And the most expensive pack might not necessarily be the best one for you."

John already knew the most expensive one wouldn't be the best one for him, but he tried to listen patiently while Yoni launched into his lecture on the philosophy of backpacks. We began to understand that this expedition to the mall might take longer than anticipated.

"Who's first?" Yoni asked. "By the way, John, that one you've chosen is a ladies' pack."

"Okay, Jupe, you go ahead," John offered.

Yoni stepped behind me and began by examining my back. Then he took two packs off the wall. "Let's try these."

After tugging on three sets of straps, hoisting the pack on my shoulders, pulling it down on my hips, taking it off, putting a twenty-kilo sandbag in the bottom, and trying it on again, and then going through the same procedure with the second one, I was asked to tell which one felt most comfortable. It happened to be the cheaper of the two.

Then the whole process began again with John. I could tell that John would rather have skipped this whole operation, but he gamely carried on and also chose the cheaper one. Two hours after entering the shop, we walked out with our new backpacks. We would need two more trips to the mall to complete our camping outfit.

After we had our gear, I wanted to practice with it. I told John I needed a trail that went uphill. One of my fears was hiking up mountains while carrying a lot of weight.

John decided that we would do two things at once. The following morning we would hike up the steep streambed of Nahal Netafim, a serious test, and we would bury some water bottles near the top. At the end of our first day on the Trail we could pick them up, thus allowing us to carry less weight. Not far from our home, this was a hike we knew well.

John carried five water bottles and our lunch in his pack, thirteen kilos altogether. There was nothing else needed for a day hike so I filled my pack with books, and found that it weighed twelve kilos.

"You know what?" I told John. "I heard Yonatan and his friends talking about marches in the army and that each soldier carries a percentage of his body weight. Sounds logical to me. So that means you'll carry 50 percent more weight than me."

John is quick with math, but he ignored my suggestion.

"Uh huh," he responded, not offering to take any of my books.

Our route began to go uphill immediately. When I had tried my pack on in the store, I didn't remember it pulling so much on my shoulders.

"Maybe I don't have it adjusted right," I told John. "How's yours?"

John was huffing. "I think I'll take out a couple of these bottles and leave them here. We don't need so much water anyway."

We managed to keep going, although I frequently had to remind John to slow down. "I can't keep up with you," I complained. "Why don't you just take some of these books?"

"Uh huh."

We thought we were familiar with Nahal Netafim, having hiked it many times; however we had always begun at the top. I had forgotten the numerous vertical climbs to circumvent the *mapalim*, dry waterfalls. We proceeded slowly and I was learning that step by step, I was able to do it.

We came to a natural chute created by water when it rushes down the *wadi*. Descending was never a problem—it's like going down a playground slide. But going up looked impossible. We took off our backpacks, a welcome respite, and somehow succeeded in pushing them up first. Then, bracing ourselves with our hands and feet, we squirmed up after them. When the top came off one of our water bottles, we felt we were heading the wrong direction on a water slide. I had to laugh as we found ourselves contorted in ridiculous positions trying to squirm up the slick rocks.

"This is nonsense," declared John. "I'm not as young as I used to be."

We reached the top and buried the water bottles under some rocks, hoping and praying that we would remember where we hid them when we passed this way in a couple of weeks.

Four hours after leaving home we reached the road with a feeling of accomplishment. We tried calling our daughter, Moriah, to ask her to come and pick us up, but there was no cell reception so we began hitch-hiking the twenty minutes back to Eilat. Before long we had a ride in a delivery truck that drove us to our home.

I felt we had passed another test, since we would probably be doing a lot of hitching on the Trail.

Things were coming together, and we still had three weeks before Jim was due to arrive.

"You know what, Jupe?" John said. "I'm thinking—according to our calculations, it's going to take us at least forty-five days to walk the *Shvil*. But Jim can stay for only a month. So what if we start next week, go out for three days, come home for the weekend when they need us most around here, do the same the following week, and then when Jim gets here, we'll really take off."

"What?" I was caught by surprise. "You mean we won't hike it continuously?"

"Look," John said, "if we hike for the month that Jim's here, we'll reach someplace in Galilee, and then if we have to come home, we'll have to go all the way back up there to complete the trip. But if we do a few sections around Eilat first, it won't involve so much traveling."

"Yeah, I get what you mean," I conceded. "But I'm not sure I'm ready, and I always envisioned just doing it straight through." It was hard for me to shift my thinking. I'm not such a spontaneous or flexible person as John is.

"What do you care?" John was persuasive. "And anyway, this way we can also try out our equipment before we leave for good. I already asked Moriah and she said that she could manage the hostel alone until Jim comes."

I understood that on this occasion I should accept John's judgment, and that I was as ready as I'd ever be, so I agreed.

"Okay, we'll start on Tuesday," John declared.

# 4. Beginning Steps & a 14-K Climb

"I hope we haven't forgotten anything." John looked at our stuff spread over the living room. "How many Bibles do you think I should take—you know, to give away to people we'll be meeting?"

"I don't know. I'm really trying to scale back," I said, wondering how we would carry all our gear. We were planning to get an early start in the morning.

"Don't worry, I've invited some guys from the hostel to go with us tomorrow—Maxim, Haile, Jordan, Tomas, Bert and his friend. They'll help carry our packs up Nahal Gishron." For most of our first day on the Trail we would be ascending this deep crevice that divides the Eilat Mountains from the Sinai; Egypt from Israel.

"That should help." But later as I lay in bed, I couldn't sleep. My heart wouldn't slow down, and my mind kept racing ahead. The next night we'd be sleeping in our little tent in Nahal Netafim, where we had hidden water bottles. Our bed was warm and soft. What would it be like, sleeping on thin pads on the ground? Would the sleeping bags be warm enough? I hoped we would manage with all the weight. John's pack weighed about twenty kilos and mine weighed fifteen, heavier than we had carried on our practice hike. The small igloo-shaped tent we bought looked simple when Yoni demonstrated it in his shop, but we hadn't tried putting it up ourselves yet. Would we manage?

The walking poles I bought pleased me. They help to take the pressure off my knees, especially going downhill. They were expensive, but a worthwhile investment. I couldn't persuade John to buy a set for himself, though. He said he liked having his hands free and wasn't coordinated enough. True, the few times we tried Israeli folk dancing, he never could negotiate the steps and kept stepping on my toes. But using walking poles didn't require the greatest coordination in the world, and they would help him with his knees. I would let him try mine and maybe afterwards he would want to buy a set.

My mind kept going into reverse mode, reviewing the events of the past few weeks, such as on Saturday when our congregation had prayed for us. We were setting out on our first stage of the Israel Trail, and I had no doubt that we needed lots of prayer.

I said good-bye to my friends at the gym. Now I would have a chance to test all my aerobic workouts and leg lifts.

When we went to the camping store to pick up a few last items, Avi, the young salesman, told us he had walked the complete *Shvil* three times. Finally we found someone who could share his experience with us. Till then we had assumed we'd begin in the north, though I was concerned that it might be cold and rainy in Galilee in the month of February. Avi said that when he had walked it in the winter, he had donned a wetsuit for going through the *wadis* flooded with winter rains. In Eilat people use wetsuits for scuba diving; so carrying them on a camping trip sounded absurd. But how would we manage to cross the rushing streams, some of them filled with freezing water from melted snow? We could skip those parts of the Trail, but I felt it was important to do it all—I didn't want to miss a thing.

Then someone at the store asked us, "Why are you hiking

from north to south? Why not from south to north?" Instantly, John and I understood the wisdom of his suggestion. In February it wouldn't be hot yet in the desert, and by the time we arrived in Galilee in March, the rains should be over. It was a mental switch for me; I'd have to forfeit our friends waiting and cheering for us at the finish line.

John was gently snoring. I eventually fell asleep.

At 8 A.M. the next morning Moriah, our youngest daughter, drove John and me, Maxim, Haile, Jordan, Tomas, Bert and Paul to Taba, the Trail's starting point, a ten minute drive from our home. We were on our way. The weather was perfect, not too hot or too cold. Fluffy white clouds decorated the sky. Moriah snapped the requisite photos of us starting, a group shot and one of John and me waving good-bye, in front of the large Trail sign. I took out the map and spread it on the ground.

"We know this place," John protested. "Put the map away and let's get going."

A few weeks previously we had come out here to practice the first few kilometers. We had hiked down Nahal Gishron, a long, deep crevice, many times; so we knew the trail started with a steady climb. With a beginning such as this, no wonder that 90 percent of the *Shvil* walkers start in the north. I soon found myself near the end of the line of hikers snaking our way up the rocky path. Only Paul, a friend of Bert's, was behind me. He was a smoker who clearly wasn't in the best shape, but coming from Amsterdam he was lured by the opportunity to encounter the desert.

Maxim and Haile sprinted off. Maxim has the physique of a body-builder; in the Ukraine he was a national Judo champion. Haile, from Eritrea, is short and slender, not someone you would imagine to be strong or a fast walker. When the war broke out between Ethiopia and Eritrea, he was forced to flee and walked on foot to Israel. It took him four months, and he carried no passport, no money, and no clothes. All he had was faith that God would take care of him and bring him to Israel. In Egypt there were many secret police, but Haile, who speaks Arabic and wore a headscarf and *jalabiya* (Bedouin man's clothing), passed himself off as a Muslim. With the help of an Ethiopian in Cairo who specializes in smuggling people, Haile contacted Sinai Bedouins, who helped him cross the border into Israel. (The long Egyptian-Israeli border passes through untamed, mountainous territory making it impossible for the Israel army to seal it hermetically.) The last day and a half of his journey he spent wrapped in a sheet, stuffed into the back of a van.

Arriving in Tel Aviv he asked an Ethiopian man on the street for information about the land. He was told that in Eilat there would be plenty of work. Haile eventually received status as a political refugee, and while he waits for a country to accept him, he works in a hotel in Eilat and comes to visit the Shelter. He's soft-spoken, and when asked if he was happy to go on the hike with us, he flashed his bashful smile, pointed up the hill and said, "Fast, fast, fast!"

I wondered how I would manage—carrying a backpack, walking up steep hills, and trying to keep up with seven men. But there was nothing I could do—I couldn't walk any faster. After ten minutes Haile looked back and stopped.

"I carry your pack," he said, motioning for me to take it off.

"Are you sure?" I asked.

"And I'll take John's," Maxim offered.

Relieved of the weight, I felt much freer, although I knew that these twenty-year-olds could still walk much faster than I. The packs didn't slow Maxim and Haile down at all—Haile was like a racehorse let out of his stable after having been cooped up all winter. The smile on his face said it all.

Our starting place was a few hundred meters from the border with Egypt, and at the top of our first hill we walked by rolls of barbed wire.

"How did you manage to climb over this?" I asked Haile.

"Went under," he replied.

After an hour of walking we reached the top of Har Zefahot. (*Har* means "mountain.") It is 278 meters above sea level, the first of numberless hills on our path.

We were rewarded with an extraordinary view of the Gulf of Eilat and the Mountains of Edom. I took out my map. Following a brief pause to catch our breath and take pictures, John took off quickly.

"Wait a minute!" I called. "You're not on the Trail." We had been following the white, blue and orange striped signs for the Israel Trail, and at this point we had come to a junction with two other trails.

"What does it matter?" John yelled back, continuing on in the same direction. "We'll meet the Israel Trail again farther down. I know this area."

"Sure," I acknowledged. "But I just like to stay on the Trail."

We had only been hiking for an hour, but I could visualize this conflict repeating itself. I like to follow directions, to abide by rules, to stay exactly on the path. John is the opposite; he doesn't like to be boxed in, and never reads instruction books. There was no use arguing with him, though, and I realized it didn't really matter.

Going down the hill I walked effortlessly; in fact, scrambling down rocks on a slope, I was faster than John. But Paul still lagged behind. Although he struggled with balance, he declined the offer of my poles. We came to another trail junction, and I produced the map. One path led back to Eilat, but our route continued through a *wadi* and up another hill.

John told Bert to take Paul back to Eilat. Bert, a volunteer in the Shelter, had been on many staff trips and could go on others in the future. We knew that we had a long day ahead of us, and this hike was obviously beyond Paul's capabilities. After making sure that Bert and Paul had enough water and understood the way back, we continued at a faster pace.

After three hours we reached the top of a ridge. To the left we could see the Egyptian border posts; to the right was Eilat in the distance. Suddenly we noticed a single hiker coming towards us with a bulky backpack.

"Shalom!" We stopped and greeted one another. I noticed that his pack was the same make as mine, except that his looked grubby and beat-up and mine was shining new.

When John asked him where he was coming from, he smiled and seemed pleased to talk. He answered that he was on the Israel Trail and would be finishing in a few hours.

We couldn't believe our luck; we had a chance to get up-to-date information.

"How long did it take you? What about water? How did you manage for supplies here in the south? Which maps do you have?" Our questions came pouring out. Actually, I was the one asking, since I had done the planning. John had no problems and no questions. When someone asked us, "Did you plan a lot for this trip?" John answered, "No, not at all," meaning, no, he didn't plan, Judy did the organizing. Whereas I enjoyed researching questions about backpacking food and equipment on the Internet, this was drudgery to John. He specialized in making decisions on the spot and instinctively knew the correct way to proceed.

The hiker, named Arnon, was from a *kibbutz* on the Golan Heights and told us that he had been hiking for a month and a half, the time we reckoned we would need. He said the *Shvil* had changed since the Israel Trail book had been published. The old trail used to go along the highway for long stretches in the south, but the new segments went through the mountains, making the trip longer. Arnon told us that water was a problem here in the desert and that he had to leave the Trail every couple of days and hitchhike to settlements to replenish his supply. We invited him to come to our hostel when he arrived in Eilat.

"What's its name?" he asked.

"The Shelter," John replied, producing a card from his backpack. "You can stay the first night for free."

"Unbelievable!" Arnon responded. "I met a guy at the monastery in Latrun who already gave me your card." Latrun was about halfway along our route.

Maxim, Jordan and Tomas told Arnon that they expected to see him later at the Shelter, and we all continued on our way. Arnon headed south to complete the Trail, and we went north.

The news about the changes in the Trail made me uneasy because I had memorized the old route. Still, I decided not to think about it for now, but resolved that when we arrived home after these first three days, I would try to find out more.

As the trail became steeper and we had to shimmy up a rock chimney, I thanked God for our personal sherpas, Haile and Maxim. I doubted this section was ever hiked from south to north, except by people walking the Israel Trail.

We finally completed our fourteen kilometers and emerged onto the road. Soon Moriah drove up as planned. The guys piled into the van, and John and I hefted the packs onto our backs.

The sun was low and the shadows were long as we descended into Nahal Netafim. The enormity of our undertaking struck me—alone in nature with only what we carried on our backs to sustain and protect us. Physically we were not far from the road, but the distance separating us from our ordinary lives was enormous. Would we find the water bottles we had hidden a few weeks ago on our practice hike? We had another day and a half till we reached Timna Park, the next outpost of civilization.

"Over here, Jupe," John called out. "I buried them behind this old barrel." We thanked God that the five water bottles were intact, even though I didn't welcome the added kilos pressing on my shoulders.

"Gotta do something about all this weight when we go out next time," John said. "This is nonsense."

As we began looking for a place to camp—out of the wind and with soft ground—we were surprised to hear voices at this late hour. Four young guides from the Field School were looking for an old marker. Field Schools, scattered throughout Israel, are a combination of visitor's center, ranger station, and guest house. The guides were ready to turn around and head home, when they spotted us. I was always eager for information and asked them about changes in the Trail.

They told me that if I came to the Field School, one of their advisers could help me. First Arnon, and then these guides—I felt that God had sent us messengers to encourage us on our first day. It was fun to meet people hiking the *Shvil* in the other direction. Would we keep meeting many people as we went along?

It was January 18 and we knew darkness fell at 5:30 P.M., even earlier in the *wadi* with its imposing walls. Just in time we found the perfect spot to camp—a sandy alcove. The tent went up surprisingly smoothly and we zipped the sleeping bags together and placed them inside. We were soon sitting cozily next to our small fire, the twigs crackling and flames dancing in the air.

"Jupe, get a picture of this; set the camera on the self-timer."

I unpacked my food bag. "What do you want for dinner, Thai noodles or Indian curry and vegetables?"

John emptied water into our small pot and dumped in the contents of the package. "Let's go for the noodles tonight."

"Wait," I said. "Let me read the instructions. You didn't measure the water and you're supposed to put a lid on while it cooks for five minutes."

"Who's going to care?"

We laughed together at our cooking efforts. The noodles tasted better than any meal I cooked at home and they nearly filled the hole in my stomach that came from climbing all day. According to the directions, the package was meant for three people. Thankfully we still had one granola bar left for dessert.

We were lying on our backs and looking up at the stars. I felt much calmer today than I had yesterday at this time. Our first day was a success, thanks to Haile and Maxim. We never could have made it up that long ascent carrying our own packs.

Besides a couple of satellites, pinpoints of light advancing steadily across the sky, and the faint glimmer of lights from Eilat, there was nothing here that was man-made. Total silence encircled us. Being out like this, I felt alive, in the way that I feel tingly and fresh when I dive into cold water.

"I'm cold," I said.

"Yeah, let's get into our sleeping bags and try out our new headlamps. We can read for a while."

In a few minutes the Bible fell out of John's hands. It was only 6:30 P.M., but we'd had a long day.


When you fall asleep at 7 P.M., you wake up early. Sleeping on a pad one centimeter thick is not the same as sleeping on your mattress at home, although we were more comfortable than we expected. Nevertheless, by 3 A.M. we had already slept for eight hours, and as I rolled from back to side to the other side, I was aware of my hips and shoulder bones pressing on the ground. We forced ourselves to stay in bed until the first rays of light, but by 5:30 John was ready to start. Unzipping the flap, he crawled out of the tent and within a few minutes had a fire burning. I wasn't eager to exchange my cozy sleeping bag for the nippy morning air, but John gave me no choice.

"Tea's ready," he announced. "Gotta get going."

Today would be the real test—on our own with heavy backpacks. The first hour was a gentle downhill walk and the cool air was refreshing. I entered into a steady rhythm—step, pole, step, pole. In my daydreams, this was how I imagined our walk—soaking up the solitude and the peacefulness of nature. Free from the cares of our everyday life. No responsibilities except to stay alive and to find a camping place every night. Unattached to earthly belongings with everything we needed in our backpacks. Finally our dream was coming true.

Then began the climb up two mountains, Har Amir and Ma'ale Amram. We had hiked often in this area, but now I was viewing the scenery with different eyes. How could we ever climb them with our heavy packs? The mountains looked imposing from a distance. I remembered leading a youth group up Har Amir. The teenagers complained the whole way, and asked every five minutes, "Are we almost there?"

John's hip and my shoulders were hurting. When Yoni adjusted my pack for me, pulling on one strap and loosening the other, I felt fine walking around his store. I remembered commenting that with such a good system of straps, I didn't even feel the weight. Ascending the mountain was another story, and now I felt every kilo. The waist belt rubbed raw spots on my skin. Perhaps I should put more weight on my shoulders, but wasn't the weight supposed to be carried on the hips? Would a couple of band aids help?

We had no choice but to go on, step by step, resting frequently. Every step was an effort. I was panting and my heart was hammering. This was harder than anything I had ever done in my life. *My friends at the gym should see me now*, I thought.

Having plenty of time alone with my thoughts, I concluded that in life we also have mountains to climb. When we look at them from far away and concentrate on how tall they are, they seem impossible to climb, but as we go up gradually, in the end we reach the summit. Then it all seems worthwhile and we're glad we didn't remain in the valley.

Every time I looked back I was surprised to see how far we

had come. After two hours of steady climbing, the ground flattened out. The Gulf of Eilat spread below us in the distance looking like a shiny blue tongue stretching out between the brown mountains. At the tip of the tongue were Eilat and Aqaba, Jordan's port city, separated by an empty stretch of no-man's land. South of Aqaba was the Saudi Arabian town of Haql, just over the border, and the Sinai coast of Egypt was visible beyond Eilat—four countries within a radius of twenty kilometers. A strong wind swirled my hair, and dark clouds blew across the sky. I felt my spirit being lifted as well.

The word for "wind" in Hebrew, *ruach*, is the same as the word for "spirit." Jesus, speaking in Hebrew, made a play on words when he used *ruach* twice in one verse in the gospel of John. "The wind blows wherever it pleases. You hear its sound, but you cannot tell where it comes from or where it is going. So it is with everyone born of the Spirit (Jn. 3:8)."

Invigorated, I looked again at the gathering clouds. "Think it could rain?" I asked.

"Nah, it never rains in Eilat."

"Let's take a picture."

"And keep moving."

"Hope we'll find our water where we buried it in Dikleh Raham."

Near the top, as we sprawled out to rest, we met a high-school class of religious boys.

"We're on the Israel Trail," John announced to a friendly trio.

"Well done!" one responded. We would be hearing that many times in the course of our walk.

*Hey, we just started*, I thought. *We haven't accomplished anything yet.* I was reminded of when Ahab, the king of Israel told Ben Hadad, the king of Syria, "One who puts on his armor should not boast like one who takes it off."

Going down on the other side, I decided that long descents

were also laborious with a heavy pack, but at least I wasn't huffing and I didn't feel my heart pounding in my chest. Half an hour later we were digging up our second cache of water bottles. A few weeks earlier we had driven out with our jeep and carried six bottles up to this stunning oasis, one of the only places in the Eilat mountains with palm trees. I pulled out a granola bar to celebrate, but with many kilometers to go, we were soon back on the path.

Once we entered the broad Nahal Raham, one of the wider streambeds in our area, we began looking for a camping spot. We searched for a place on the *wadi*'s side to protect us from the wind, but also to be on higher ground in case it rained. It was already drizzling when we put our tent up, in spite of John's prediction. Indian curry was the main course tonight, with a cucumber, carrot, apple, and a granola bar completing our dinner. While we ate, we were treated to a spectacular sunset. The gray blue colors of the clouds were a backdrop for the golden hills in front of us.

I reflected that many people dream about getting out into nature for a few hours and are willing to pay well for the experience. We were going to be here for days on end.

John stretched out next to our fire. We still couldn't really grasp that we were finally here. It was so quiet that my ears strained to hear a sound, and all I could hear was a kind of ringing inside my head.

The rain began to fall harder.

"Wonder if there's room for our packs inside the tent," John said.

"I can't believe it." This didn't fit into my plans. "Five times a year it rains in Eilat, and we get one of those times our second night on the Trail."

"Let's move our stuff inside. Now we'll be able to see how well the tent works. I'm going to use my pack as a pillow."

John maneuvered his pack under his head and in a half-sitting position announced, "Hey, this is really comfortable." Because my legs were not as long as his, I placed my bag under my feet and managed to more or less stretch out. We looked at our watches, found it was only 6:20 P.M., and we were already tucked into bed. It had been a long day. We had walked about seventeen kilometers, tackled several steep climbs, and carried our own loads for the first time.

Thankfully, it didn't rain hard, and next morning the path looked promisingly easy—a flat, slightly downhill jeep trail. We soon discovered, however, that hiking on a jeep track had its own difficulties. Marching on the gravel surface required extra effort, like walking on a sandy beach, and we found ourselves trudging over the rough stones next to the road.

"Look, here's the gate that's marked on the map," I said after an hour.

We had entered the territory of the Timna Copper Mines with its huge slag piles and artificial craters.

"Wow, I remember when this place was a beehive of activity," John remarked, "and look at it now. Not a person or truck to be seen." The modern copper industry had flourished here until the price of copper decreased in the 1970s.

Ever since the sixth millennium B.C., when it is believed that man devised a system to turn rough stones into pliable metal, copper had been mined and smelted in the Timna Valley. Because of its use in bronze, copper was an important metal in antiquity, and Timna is the oldest known center of copper production. Mining activities reached a peak during the reign of the Pharaohs from the fourteenth to the twelfth centuries B.C., when Egyptian mining expeditions together with the Midianites and local Amalekites turned the Timna Valley into a large-scale copper industry. In the 1930s the famous archaeologist, Nelson Glueck, declared that King Solomon had mined at Timna and named the site King Solomon's Mines, arousing much worldwide interest. But later field work yielded no evidence of mining activity in Solomon's time. A Victorian novel called *King Solomon's Mines* adds to the exotic connection between Solomon and Timna and to the confusion, because the best-selling book is set in Africa.

The refinery appeared to be located in one of the most uninviting, desolate places imaginable. Archeologists, however, have discovered that the site was chosen in ancient times to take advantage of the strong winds that blow down the Arava Valley. Furthermore, the surrounding cliffs were useful not only for protection from enemies, but also to keep the slaves who worked the mines in a sort of prison camp.

An easy climb over a hill brought us into Timna National Park, located in a U-shaped valley surrounded by yellow sandstone mountains. Timna is remarkable for the amazing sandstone formations, created by erosion, which are given names such as "pillars, arches, tables, and mushrooms." The streaks of turquoise-colored rocks and the blue-green pebbles scattered on the ground were evidence of the copper in the area.

"Look Jupe—9:30 A.M.!" John exclaimed. "Took us twenty-five hours of walking to get here. We walked to Timna! Can you believe it? Let's stop for a break in the Bedouin tent."

Black netting, cushions on the floor, low tables, and the smell of pita baking—the Bedouin tent was a welcome sight after three days in the wilderness. We collapsed on the pillows and enjoyed a snack of pita and *lebaneh* (sour milk cheese) with unlimited quantities of sweet mint tea. The best part was eating something that we hadn't cooked ourselves and talking to someone other than each other.

The rest of the day's hike over flat-topped Mt. Timna in the middle of the park would have been strenuous if we hadn't left our packs with a friend who worked at the park. We hiked up with only one water bottle each. Since this was the end of our first section, he would drive our packs home for us. I nearly skipped up that mountain, like one of the ibexes we had encountered yesterday, who seem to defy gravity as they leap over hills.

With Mt. Timna conquered, we tramped to the highway, waited at the bus stop, and a cab with one passenger picked us up. We were on our way home.

Smelly and filthy, we climbed into the taxi. "We're on the *Shvil*," we announced. I felt, after three days on the Trail, that we had earned the right to make this public declaration.

# 5. Command Cars &
# Moon Shadows

Having arrived home early from Timna, I jumped into the car and drove to the Field School. The information I gathered from fellow hikers on our trip about the changes in the Trail troubled me, and I wanted to know what to expect.

"There have been three major changes to the *Shvil* here in the south," the friendly guide at the Nature Authority informed me as we bent over the maps laid out on his desk. He painstakingly marked out the new trails on my maps in a line of blue dots. For the sections unfamiliar to him, he phoned a colleague.

"You can choose to take the old route or the new ones. Everyone creates his own Israel Trail. There are still thirty kilometers that parallel the highway. I'd skip that part if I were you."

*What?* I thought. *Omit part of the Israel Trail? Create my own Israel Trail?*

For someone like me who likes to follow rules, to make lists, and to check things off, the idea of a trail with many variations was disturbing.

Weekends in the Shelter Hostel and in our congregation are busy. It was important for John and me to be home for the upcoming few weekends since Jim, John's replacement, hadn't arrived yet. Furthermore, we needed the time to regroup, rethink, repack, and be refreshed. I made a list in my diary of things I had learned from our first three days:

- *Pack lighter.*
- *We can do it.*
- *Two bottles of water are needed a day.*
- *We meet nice people on the Trail.*
- *Our sleeping pads are okay.*

Three days later, on the eve of our second journey on the Israel Trail, I lay in bed. I was excited to leave again, but thankfully I didn't have trouble falling asleep. I knew I could walk with a pack and that our gear was warm enough. I knew that I ached but not too much.

We got an earlier start this time, leaving home at 6 A.M. to begin the next stage of our journey. Maxim, the athlete, and Saul from Argentina were our sherpas this time, and Bert came along for the hike. We began where we had left off, at the entrance to Timna Park, and climbed up a steep ridge that formed the boundary of Timna Valley.

I had to rest frequently to catch my breath, and each time I looked down into the semi-circular valley, I had a better view of the fantastic rock formations rising above the red, yellow, orange, brown and black sand. Maxim and Saul practically ran with our packs the two hours to the top, where the land flattened out. It felt good to be moving my body again, to be using all my muscles. I loved the whoosh of the wind in my ears and the cloud shadows drifting over the landscape.

By 10 A.M. it was time to part with our companions. The three men would hike down the cliff into the park another way, and we would continue north. After explaining to them which trails to follow and showing them carefully on the map, we waved good-bye, took some photos and forged ahead on our own.

"Look, Jupe." John said. "Do you see those shapes on that hill in the distance?"

They appeared to be an immense distance away.

"That must be Mitzpe Ramon."

"You're kidding. No, it can't be," I asserted. "We'll only get there on our tenth day."

"Anyway, can you believe we can walk all the way to Mitzpe?" John continued. "Unbelievable."

I was positive we were seeing an army outpost much closer than Mitzpe Ramon, but I learned that when I focus on the horizon it seems impossible that we'll ever reach that far. I have learned to concentrate on where I'm going that day and then the next day after that, and eventually I'll reach my goal.

For years we had hiked around Eilat and the area was familiar. We were especially delighted when, after lunch, we walked on a trail that was new to us and enjoyed the surprise of finding new sights around every bend.

John pointed to a spot of green in the Arava Valley. "You can see the Experimental Station from here, where I used to work."

He was referring to the early 1970s, when he first came to Israel, and he worked for a number of years in agriculture. Growing up in a small coastal town in Holland, John's first attraction had been to the sea, and at age eighteen he joined the Merchant Marines and was later inducted into the Royal Dutch Marines.

After four years John was tired of military discipline and longed to be free. He joined the ranks of the thousands of young people from all over the world who came to Israel to work in *kibbutzim*. At that time swarms of backpackers were roaming the planet seeking more than a change of scenery and interesting museums. As idealists, they were searching for an alternative lifestyle. Many found on the *kibbutz* an opportunity to live as part of a community while receiving room and board and excursions around the country in exchange for healthy outdoor work.

John chose a *kibbutz* in the sunny south of Israel where driving a tractor in the spacious wheat fields of the Negev desert was like a dream come true. He was sure that on the *kibbutz* he had found the perfect society, a socialistic system where everyone was equal. But after two years in which he learned Hebrew and made many Israeli friends, John began to see that although everyone was supposedly equal, some were more equal than others. John was impressed to observe that elections were held every year for the *kibbutz* secretary, treasurer, and other positions, but after a time he noticed that the secretary became the treasurer, and the treasurer became the work manager; the power stayed in the hands of a small group of people.

Disillusioned, John left the *kibbutz* and went down to Eilat. He settled in with a group of hippies who were living in home-made shacks on the outskirts of town. They worked occasionally, smoked dope, philosophized about the meaning of life, and dreamed about further travels.

The restlessness inside him was growing, but he found that getting high didn't satisfy him or fill the void inside. Then one of his friends gave John a Bible. As a Catholic boy growing up in Holland, he had never actually read the Bible, although he'd gone to Mass, confession, and learned some prayers in Latin. John devoured the Bible and found answers to his questions: "What's the purpose of life? What am I doing here and where am I going?" He put his trust in Jesus and his life was radically changed.

Certain that all his old friends and family would be as eager to embrace his new faith as he was, John began sharing with everyone the good news he had found. John sensed that God had a long-term purpose for him in Israel, and prayed that God would give him a Jewish wife, which would allow him to immigrate to Israel. I was the answer to his prayers, and we married in 1975.

After the Sinai was given back to Egypt in 1980 and we moved permanently to Eilat, John found a job at the Agricultural

Experimental Station for the southern Arava region. John was appointed field manager, thanks to his experience on the *kibbutz*. He ran around all day barefoot in the sand, drove the tractor and enjoyed the peaceful surroundings with the rocky mountains of Edom as a backdrop. When after five years he hurt his back and could no longer drive the tractor and bend over to pick tomatoes, God opened the door for us to begin the Shelter Hostel.

Now as we walked, delighting in the spectacular views of the Arava Valley, the afternoon passed quickly. Towards evening we found a *wadi* with an abundance of low scrubby bushes and two acacia trees. The acacia, the most common tree in the south of Israel, is perfectly suited to its desert environment. The small leaves help to conserve water; the long tap root bores deep into the earth, and a second set of roots spreads out widely just under the ground's surface. Because of its slow growth, the wood is hard and dense, making it a prized fuel for Bedouins.

We always tried to camp in the shade of an acacia tree, although because of its thorns we had to be careful handling its branches or walking around barefoot underneath it. Sometimes as I looked out over a landscape of acacia trees with their umbrella-like crowns, I imagined that I was in the African savanna and expected to see a couple of giraffes come striding up to munch the leaves, or zebras grazing nearby. In Israel we are more likely to see ibexes, with their backward curved horns, climbing up an acacia tree like animal acrobats and nibbling the foliage. Or we might see camels contentedly browsing, their floppy lips impervious to the barbs.

Called *shittah* in Hebrew, the acacia was used for constructing and furnishing the Tabernacle in the wilderness, where God chose to meet with man. It's hard to see how boards could be made from this gnarled, twisted, and prickly tree. Yet after being hewn, the boards were overlaid with gold. I thought of how God had taken a prickly and crooked plank like me, smoothed me out, covered me with the gold of obedience, and made me useful for Him.

We sprawled out under the larger of the two acacias and had a welcome cup of smoky mint tea. Thai noodles filled our hungry stomachs, a granola bar satisfied my sweet tooth, and we felt at peace with the world. The time came to put up the tent before the darkness fell.

John had been worried about the tent from the beginning. He doesn't like gadgets, reading instructions, or anything that takes more than a few minutes to do. His idea of a tent is a tarp hung over some poles. Amazingly, however, the first two nights the tent had gone up without a glitch. Perhaps we had become careless, but this time the poles kept getting twisted, the tent ended up inside out, and it was a total mess.

"Okay, let's pray," John said.

"God, help us set up this tent. It's getting dark and cold."

So we tried again, from the beginning.

"Look, hold the pole like this, press here, and at the same time give a pull," John directed.

"I'm trying. Maybe you better take my side." We were careful not to accuse each other.

"No big deal," John said. "We can just sleep outside."

I could tell it was going to be a cold night and I didn't relish sleeping under the stars. "Let's pray again," I said. I felt like crying.

"Can't we just sleep in it like this?" John proposed.

"Inside out?" I tried to remain calm.

Suddenly I remembered—I had the directions to the tent in my jacket pocket. I had nearly thrown them out, thinking that we knew how to erect the tent by now, and I had forgotten about them.

The assembly instructions were divided into four steps with accompanying pictures. I read aloud step one: "Grasp the lanyard at the peak of the tent."

"What's a lanyard?" asked John.

"Look, it's this little loop," I said, laughing. I thought it was funny that John had lived fifty-nine years without knowing what a lanyard was.

"Well, what is it for, anyway?"

"It's to give us something to pull. But somehow we have our tent inside out and the lanyard is on the inside of the tent instead of outside," I said. "How did we do it so completely wrong?" In another ten minutes, our shelter for the night was secure. We paused to thank God for it.

The next morning we were up early as usual and in a few hours we came out on a road, where a thirty-kilometer stretch of the *Shvil* paralleled the highway. As much as I didn't want to miss any part of the Trail, walking next to the road would be boring, and our time was limited. We began hitchhiking while we walked. Up until the mid-1970s in Israel it was common to see hoards of hitchhikers. No one feared hitchhiking or picking up travelers. Our preferred method of traveling then was to stick out our hand and flick it up and down from the wrist, Israeli style. Now that it isn't common anymore (as in most countries, people are afraid of either being picked up by a crackpot or letting one in their car) we wondered how easy it would be for two dirty, middle-aged people with large backpacks to get a lift. Surely we didn't look like terrorists or psychopaths, though.

We were on a road with almost no traffic, but I spotted a few cars in the distance.

"They're army, not allowed to pick up civilians," John said.

Three vehicles pulled to a stop in front of us and the officer stuck his head out of the window.

"Shalom! We're on the Israel Trail," John explained. "We're trying to get to the next intersection, five Ks down the road."

"Okay," said the officer, "we'll take you, but if a military police car passes us, duck."

Several soldiers jumped out and rearranged themselves among the vehicles. They told me to sit in the front seat of one jeep, while John went in the other jeep, and our packs ended up being thrown in the back of the command car.

The officer's name was Moshe. He and his companions were friendly young men, on patrol near the Egyptian border. Picking up hitchhikers relieved their boredom.

They dropped us off at the Naot Smadar Inn, an organic restaurant specializing in home-cooked food prepared from products grown and raised at the settlement across the road. We suggested they have a drink with us in the restaurant, but they declined. So we gave them cards from the Shelter, invited them to visit us, and wished them well.

We felt civilized sitting on chairs and eating at a table after having carefully washed our hands. The minestrone soup and Greek salad with fresh goat cheese was one of the most delicious meals I had ever tasted. The waitress informed us that the next bus would pass by in another hour and a half, so we went out to the road and began hitching.

A car going the opposite direction stopped and the window rolled down. "I have some business to do on a *kibbutz* up the road," the driver said, "but if you're still here in half an hour, I'll take you."

Since few cars used this road, we were glad to see the man, Shmuelik, again as he had promised. Even more encouraging was to discover that the spirit of hitching was still alive. He drove us twenty-five kilometers to the next intersection and from there we turned into the wilderness.

After a two-hour walk through the wide Nahal Tzichor streambed, we found a pleasant, sandy camping spot. "Okay, this time let's set up the tent first," I said, "then have our tea."

"I'm holding the lanyard," John said.

We advanced farther than I thought we would. In general, we

were moving faster than I had expected. But tomorrow we would have some challenges, up Vardit Canyon and down Barak Canyon. With drastic changes in elevation over a short distance and several five-meter ladders each, they are possibly the most arduous trails in the area.

The full moon was so bright it lit up the sky like a lighthouse. In town you often don't even notice the phase of the moon. But camping in the desert, a full moon makes all the difference.

"I remember walking on the beach in Nueiba by the light of the full moon," I reminisced. Nueiba was the beach in the Sinai where I started to read the Bible; we lived there after we immigrated to Israel.

"At the time it seemed those days would never end," John said. "You can practically read by the moonlight tonight."

It was so light that we might have had trouble falling asleep if we hadn't been so tired.

It was still dark when John began tossing around in our sleeping bag. Then I heard the tent's zipper opening. At first I tried to ignore him. "What time is it?" I muttered, half asleep.

"We've slept for nine hours already," John announced cheerfully. "It's 4 o'clock and we can walk in the moonlight."

I couldn't believe that he expected me to get up before the sun had risen. It was cold. How could I get out of my sleeping bag?

"Look, I've got a fire going already. Ready for a nice cup of tea?"

"How will we find the trail signs in the dark?" I asked, stalling.

"The moon gives a lot of light, and I was here last year with Herbby, remember?"

Sometimes I know it's not worth arguing, and I could hear the excitement in John's voice, like a little boy on a new adventure.

"How about breakfast?" he offered.

At 4 A.M. I had no appetite.

Thankfully the path was relatively smooth and the way straightforward. I warmed up as I walked and although I didn't want to admit it, there was a certain magic to hiking by the light of the full moon. When would we ever do this again?

Even my concern at missing the Vardit Canyon was unfounded, because we soon found ourselves approaching the entrance. The timing was perfect—the sun was just beginning to offer some faint light.

Although I had been here before, I couldn't help thinking that a first-time visitor to this canyon would be amazed at the beauty awaiting him. We walked through an open area with a large acacia tree in the middle and outsized boulders strewn around. Surrounded by rock walls on three sides, we seemed to be walking straight into a cliff. Suddenly a cleft opened in the cliff in front of us. In the half-darkness we followed the winding path forward and upwards through swirls of white, pink, red, purple, and yellow sandstone. The wind and rain through the years had produced incredible flowing shapes and forms in the stone. The canyon was so narrow in some places that we could reach out and touch both sides. If it had rained recently, we could have been in trouble because the hollows would have been full of water. Swimming across would have been impossible with our packs.

Snaking up the trail, we turned a corner and found ourselves standing in front of a five-meter-high ladder. Two metal cables with bars between them were pegged into the top and draped over the side of the cliff to take us over the dry waterfall. I tried to ignore the large empty pool below the ladder. Though I had climbed ladders before, I was terrified as I imagined the weight of my backpack dragging me down. John climbed up first.

"No problem! Hang on with both hands. Go slowly. Stay close to the cliff," he instructed me as he climbed.

What he meant as encouragement only increased my anxiety.

I had an idea. John would climb back down and carry my pack up, and then I would mount without the pack.

John, ever the gentleman on the trail, readily agreed, and I reached the top without difficulty.

Soon we were out of the canyon and stopped at the top for a breakfast of pita with peanut butter and coffee. After two hours of walking along the plateau, we descended into the Barak Canyon, a reverse of our ascent up Vardit.

Would my knees hold on the steep and prolonged decline? The orthopedist had said I had nothing to worry about, but I was concerned: what if I had a lot of pain? Would I be able to continue our trek?

My knee was fine, but my ankle hurt where it rubbed against my boot. I used my extra sock as an insole and we hobbled along. John's knee was now aching, and he had blisters under both feet. Before we left home, I had suggested that he use poles; now I insisted he buy a pair.

From the end of the canyon to the road was a lengthy, monotonous walk over a stony plain. No trees grew on the empty flatlands, and the sun beat down on our heads. So when a jeep stopped and offered to take us out to the highway, John quickly accepted. I didn't argue, having learned not to be a stickler for walking every single kilometer of the trail.

As we waited at the bus stop for a hitch or a bus to Eilat, I wondered what it would be like next time to leave home and not return, until we finished the trail in Kibbutz Dan, more than eight hundred kilometers away.

# 6. Traversing the Negev

At home I felt unsettled. My mind kept returning to images
and vistas of the Trail, the mountain panoramas, and our little tent
under the stars, away from civilization. I went through my daily
routine, but could hardly wait to be off again. We had to wait,
though, till the end of the week, when Jim came. We spent an
evening with him, catching up and going over the situations he
might encounter in the month ahead.

The night before we left I lay awake reviewing in my mind
all the contents of my pack and all that had to be done while we
were away. We were thrilled that our tracts had arrived, because
it was important to us to have something to give people we met
along the way.

On the front of the tract was a cheerful caricature of the two
of us against a desert background, the three-colored symbol of the
Israel Trail and the title, *Stand and Walk the Land*, taken from
God's command to Abraham in Genesis 13:17. In the short text
we explained why we were walking the Trail and who we were.
We described how we had found the peace we were searching for
through a personal relationship with God, and how the prophecies
from the Old Testament about the Messiah are fulfilled in Jesus.
In conclusion we invited the readers to contact us and to visit our
hostel at the beginning or end of their trek. The small pamphlet

wouldn't add weight to their backpacks; but it would introduce them to us and our faith.

I had mailed a package of tracts and the four maps we would need in the center of the country to our friends, Yakim and Debbie in Arad, a small city in the south of Israel, which is perched above the Dead Sea, on the border of the Negev and Judean Deserts. Arad, the first town we would cross, divided the southern uninhabited desert part of the *Shvil* from the more populated northern section.

We had given the maps for the north, and another one hundred tracts, to our oldest son Josh who was studying in Haifa. Although each map and tract in itself wasn't heavy, I was aware of every gram and was trying to cut where I could.

"If all goes as planned, we'll meet you in Haifa in about a month," I had told Josh. "It would be great if you had a day off from your studies to walk with us."

On the Internet I had found a telephone number for the Israel Trail Committee's coordinator, Danny Gaspar. He had explained to me about the new sections of the Trail and made it clear that, contrary to what we'd been told by the guide at the Eilat Field School, there was only one official Trail. I had been relieved to know that we wouldn't be deciding which version to hike as we went along.

One big change was in the Negev area between the Large and Small Craters. I had already decided we would follow the old Trail in this section because it was at least two days shorter, although the new version looked more interesting.

"We've taken away the old trail markers, or wiped them out," Danny had informed me. "Everyone has to walk the new trail now."

"Unfortunately the new path isn't marked yet on the most recent maps," he'd continued. "But don't worry, I'll fax you written directions for it." I wondered how hikers managed who didn't happen to contact him and happily set out with food and water expecting to walk the trail shown on the maps, only to find it was deleted and that they would have to hike an additional two or three days.

We started early on Thursday morning with another enthusiastic group from the hostel. This time we drove an hour and a half to return to the road at the end of the Barak Canyon where we had left off. John was well prepared with a new pair of hiking boots, walking sticks, and two elastic knee braces; he was determined to prevent any knee problems. Back on the Trail, I was delighted to be engulfed by quietness again and to return to living for the day, away from computers, cars, and all the other modern conveniences that complicate our lives.

All day we followed an easy jeep road, known as "The Springs Route." At first glance the name didn't make sense, because we didn't see any springs. Later we came to places with palm trees and reeds, and I understood that the Arava, part of the Rift Valley fault, has many springs flowing into it. The Great Rift Valley extends for some five thousand kilometers from northern Syria to Mozambique in East Africa, of which the section from the Dead Sea to the Gulf of Eilat is called the Arava, or *Wadi Araba* in Arabic.

Within hours we began to see flowers. In Israel, rain falls between October and April; in the summer the land is dry and yellow-brown. When the first rains appear, the flowers and grass awake from their slumber and poke their heads out of the sand. *Yoreh* in Hebrew means "early rain," and is a cause for joy heralded in the newspapers. With the Eilat area's miniscule rainfall, we may not see flowers even in the winter. But the north of Israel becomes a visual feast. A carpet of green covers the hills; flowers of every color appear. So the beds of bright yellow and purple flowers were both a sign of our northward advance and of adequate rain in this area.

After five hours of hiking we reached the ruins of Moa, a Nabatean city on the Spice Route, across the Arava Valley from Petra, the ancient Nabatean's capital city. The spice trade was mentioned in the biblical story of Joseph whose jealous brothers threw him into a cistern. They then sold him to a caravan of Ishmaelites whose camels were loaded with "spices, balm, and myrrh" on their way to Egypt. Nine hundred years later, about 1000 B.C., the Queen of Sheba journeyed up to meet King Solomon in Jerusalem with "a very great caravan of camels carrying spices, large quantities of gold, and precious stones" (1 Ki. 10:2).

The Nabatean civilization, with their knowledge of the secrets of the desert, controlled the spice trade for centuries. The route stretched from the Persian Gulf to Gaza from where goods were shipped to Rome. The Nabateans were a mysterious civilization whose origins, trade routes, and borders remain a puzzle. They conspired to keep their water sources hidden from their rivals and developed sophisticated systems to preserve the desert's precious water, including dams, plastered cisterns, and conduits. The Nabateans mastered the ancient economic market, employing thousands of specially-bred camels to haul items from as far away as China, India, Thailand, and Korea. Spices were the most common merchandise, but perfumes, herbs, wood, gems, silks, medicines, and metals were also exchanged. They even sold asphalt from the Dead Sea to Egypt for use in mummification, coffin-sealing, and glue. Cleopatra was notably involved in this extremely lucrative business after Marc Antony, the Roman politician and general, annexed the Nabatean kingdom around 36 B.C. and gave the Dead Sea region with its asphalt to her. Later, Christianity killed the practice of mummification because, believing in the spiritual resurrection from the dead, it was no longer necessary to preserve the physical bodies.

As entrepreneurs, the Nabateans gained tremendous profits, but not without risks from thieves, sandstorms, and other threats.

They excelled in military skills to deal with the robbers that
preyed on their trade, and in their turn exacted taxes and tolls. In
today's terms, the Nabateans were not only the truckers, they also
controlled the toll stations on the turnpikes, policed the highways,
and managed the motels and restaurants along the way. They were
a genuine mafia.

At the site of the once-prosperous city of Moa, all that remains
today are stone blocks that are the color of the surrounding sand.
A sign describes them as a fort, perched on a hill, with a *khan*, or
caravansary, at its base. After arranging ourselves on one of the
broken walls for a group photo, our friends left us and walked the
couple of kilometers out to the highway.

We found a hidden *wadi* where we could camp for the night.
I lay there feeling apprehensive about the rest of our trip. We had
some long two-day treks, and from the settlement of Sde Boker
to Arad was five days. Would we need to rest? What about the
weather? I had to trust in God.

The next morning we got an early start, and by 8:45 A.M. the trail
passed behind Mercaz Sapir, a small community where we knew
we would find a supermarket and water. John thought we might
find a tap on the outside of the village to save having to walk
into the center. He contended that we didn't need any more food,
though I had been looking forward to getting snacks and fruit in
preparation for a two-day trek across the Negev.

Sapir, only three kilometers from Jordan, is enclosed by a
fence, as are most settlements in Israel, and especially those near
borders. We walked around the perimeter fence on the south side
and, entering the village, found the small grocery store. The food
looked tempting but I knew that we were especially limited with
weight on this stretch. So I settled for two bananas, which we
ate on the spot so they wouldn't get squished in our packs, and

a few apples and granola bars. On the way out we found a water faucet near the gate. We each filled up four one-and-a-half liter bottles, and when we tried to put our packs on our backs we could barely lift them.

"Are you sure we need to take so much water?" John groaned.

"Better safe than sorry," I told him. "I'd hate to run out in a place where we aren't likely to meet anyone for two days."

Rather than returning to the trail the same way, we looked at the map and figured it would be the same distance if we followed the fence along the north side of the village. Unfortunately, however, army bases aren't marked on maps, and we soon discovered that there was a camp bordering Sapir to the north. Since John's days as a marine he hasn't liked back-tracking, so we gamely began hiking around the army base.

We were hiking farther and farther from the Trail. I didn't complain aloud, but John knew I was stressed—I became nervous when I was off the trail for long. As we slogged over the rough landscape, we found ourselves heading in the opposite direction from the one we intended. I thought about Moses and the children of Israel wandering through this wilderness. What must it have been like for Moses to have thousands of complaining, newly-freed slaves behind him? I supposed that he never went up a *wadi* only to find it was a dead end, or found himself on top of a cliff from which there was no way down. He, at least, had the pillar of cloud by day and the pillar of fire by night to lead him.

By the time we found the trail again we had been walking for at least two hours and covered six extra kilometers. I was instantly relieved to see our trail signs, though now we began a steep climb. We went up and down hills with our heavy packs and saw no one all day. By three in the afternoon I was ready to stop; we had been hiking for nine hours.

"Look at the map, Jupe," John said. "We're not far from a real campsite. We might meet people there."

"I'm wiped out, but okay," I agreed. "It's a weekend and maybe there'll be hikers or jeepists."

The Israel Trail, unlike national trails in other countries, doesn't have shelters or hostels along the route. In the nature reserves, camping is officially allowed only in designated campgrounds. But since such campgrounds are few and far between, small groups of campers generally choose their own spots to camp, and try to minimize their impact on the environment.

Coming down a steep hill, we finally reached the Zinim Cliffs Reserve. Our campsite was a sandy spot with low scrubby bushes and a cliff behind it. We were alone. As John made the fire and prepared our simple meal, I wrote in my diary some lessons I had learned that day:

- *It's important to stay on the trail.*
- *I'm not happy off the trail.*
- *If we veer off, it's best to get back on the trail as soon as possible, even to backtrack, rather than to keep going in the wrong direction.*

Several years before, I had developed the habit of looking for parallels between our walks in the desert and what happens in life. I keep a list that I call "Lessons from the Trail," and am always seeking new similitudes. This day, after straying off the Trail for over two hours, it became clear to me that as long as I stay on God's path for my life, using the Bible as my map, and my conscience as my compass, I have peace. It's easy to wander and to stumble, but then the wisest thing I can do is to quickly find my way back.

John had our meal ready, and while we ate our package of rice curry, a jeep pulled into the camp farther down. We finished our meal and strolled over to visit. A man was preparing pita and tea with his four children. He introduced himself as Amit, a farmer from the nearby cooperative village, Moshav Ein Yahav.

Seeing a family camping together reminded me of the trips we had taken with our children. Amit explained that he was waiting for two friends who began hiking at Mitzpe Ramon and had asked that he meet them here with water. We waited with Amit's family until dark, when the friends finally appeared out of the darkness.

Sitting around a campfire with other people was a change for us. Amit's friend, Ilan, was working on his doctorate in astronomy. He pointed out the stars and constellations to the children: Orion, the Big and Small Dippers, the North Star. The Milky Way looked as if a painter had taken a wide brush of white paint and swiped it across the sky, some places getting more paint and others less.

The oldest boy was fascinated, but he also had a serious question. "Who made all the stars? Do you think there's a God?"

"Well," answered Ilan, "there must be a higher power that created all this, but I don't believe in a personal God who is involved in our lives today."

"Funny," his girlfriend added, "whenever we're out camping and begin talking about stars, the subject of God comes up."

We pointed out that belief in a God who cares for each of us individually is the next logical step after acknowledging God the Creator, but the discussion didn't progress far. All of a sudden we realized that it was getting late and we should return to our tent. Enjoying the company and absorbed in the conversation, we had lost track of the time; but we'd be getting up early and had a grueling day ahead of us.

Having said good-bye, we strode into the darkness. We had left our camp in daylight; now it was pitch dark—the total darkness that is felt only in places where there is no artificial light for miles in any direction. Even when we camp in the mountains outside Eilat, we still see the shimmer of the city lights in the sky. But here, as we left the glow of the dying campfire behind us, the

only light came from the stars shining so brightly that we felt
we could reach out and touch them. We marched off confidently
enough, but within a few minutes I began to wonder if we were
heading in the right direction. I felt a tightening in my chest as
I started to panic.

"John, d'you think this is the right way? Maybe we should go
back and borrow their flashlight." I hesitated to voice my fear, but
I could sense that John was uneasy also.

I knew what John's answer would be, because whenever we
left home, John never liked to go back if we forgot something.
I realized that even a flashlight wouldn't help in our situation—it
merely lights up a small area. Nothing but a gigantic searchlight
could possibly have helped us.

We stopped to pray, thankful to have a relationship with a
God who cares.

John and I have a good sense of direction, but our tent was
miniscule in the vast desert. Suppose we kept walking in the
wrong direction? We would wander for hours. We remembered,
however, the approximate distance from our neighbor's camp to
ours, and that our tent was next to a cliff.

As we cautiously, almost blindly continued, we stumbled on
an old piece of carpet we had noticed earlier. Thank God! Finally
a familiar sign. Then we saw our tent dimly in the distance. I
felt foolish. What kind of campers were we to lose our tent? But
when we reached the tent, I had another surprise. I had taken
my sleeping mat out to sit on while we ate our dinner, and now
it was missing. The wind must have blown it away. After some
searching, John found it in the bushes. God had answered our
prayer to meet people, but we had a lot to learn about camping.


The next day we tackled some wild, treacherous terrain. We
climbed up and over three dry waterfalls and up and down Mt.

Yahav, one of the highest mountains in the area. The hiking, however, was getting noticeably easier; I didn't quake when I saw a mountain any more. Step by step by step, our muscles were strengthening and we were getting in better shape. I began to look forward to the view from the top, just as after difficult periods in my life, I appreciate being able to look back from where I've come and enjoy the victory.

The strong head wind slowed our progress and prevented us from taking a decent lunch break. But soon after lunch we encountered two men, Yaron and Boaz, sitting next to their jeep while a group of tourists were scrambling up the nearby *mapal*.

"Shalom!" John greeted them.

"Hey, are you going skiing?" Yaron chuckled when he saw our hiking poles. We were to find that 95 percent of the people we met asked this question, and each thought it was the funniest and most original joke to ask someone in the middle of the desert.

"Well, as a matter of fact, we're on our way to Mt. Hermon," John answered smiling. Mt. Hermon, Israel's only ski resort, is close to the end of the Israel Trail. "We're on the *Shvil Israel*, began in Eilat, and today's our ninth day." John pulled one of our pamphlets from the pocket of his fleece. Boaz told us he had met people like us before, Israelis who believe that Jesus is the Messiah.

In Israel, 80 percent of the population is Jewish. The remainder are mainly Arabs, of which the majority are Muslim and a small minority are Christian. In the land where Jesus was born and lived His entire life, very few Israelis believe in Him today, perhaps 10,000 out of a population of 5,600,000 Jewish Israelis. So we welcomed these opportunities along the trail to share something about our faith with people such as Yaron and Boaz.

We welcomed the cups of strong, sweet Turkish coffee that Boaz had prepared on their gas stove. Yaron invited us to visit

him at his home in Rosh Pina, a small town near the end of the
Trail. When we parted I felt a renewed surge of energy. I didn't
know whether it was from the coffee or the conversation or both.
Or maybe God?

We stopped early because we had a challenging section of
the Trail ahead of us: the first of two "cock's combs" we would
encounter on our trek. I remembered from a previous crossing
that after a steep ascent, we would be walking across a knife-
edged mountain top for two or three kilometers. Not wanting to
be trapped at a higher elevation on an exposed rock face when the
sun went down, we found a protected side canyon off the main
*wadi*, where we gathered firewood and made tea. The "cock's
comb" loomed above us, a reminder of the challenge we would
face in the morning.

We basked in the luxury of having time to lie back, read, and
rest. On our third night in a row of camping without going home, a
milestone for us, now I knew we could meet this challenge.

Why didn't more people we knew walk the *Shvil*? After nine
days, we were convinced that hiking the Israel Trail was one of the
best decisions we had ever made.

I took the time to write in my diary:

- *When on a long trip, don't push. On a short trip you
  can keep going till dark, but this is different.*
- *To do this you need:*
  ◊ *no serious health problems*
  ◊ *reasonable fitness*
  ◊ *motivation & commitment*

It was Saturday evening and we imagined our congregation in
Eilat gathering. After our meal we each picked out a chapter from
the Bible and read it aloud, and when the words on the page were
no longer legible in the darkness, we sang. At home we never took

the time for these simple pleasures—reading to one another and praising God in song, just the two of us. I wondered if we might continue some of these practices when we got home.

As the embers from our campfire faded we became aware of distant voices. When you are out in the wilderness, away from anything man-made, your senses become fine-tuned. The parched desert has few smells, so you immediately notice the scent of a special plant or of a campfire; the sound of an airplane high overhead, a jeep far away, or human voices seem loud.

We both sat up straight, instantly alert. Voices at this time of night, in the dark? Then we saw them—three figures silhouetted against the darkening sky, coming down the hill. For some reason it seemed tremendously important that they didn't pass us by.

"Let's walk out to the main *wadi* to meet them," John suggested.

"What? And risk losing our tent again? What if we don't find our way back?" I was paranoid about wandering too far away from our camping spot. I wasn't going to let the tent out of my sight.

John didn't think it would be a problem, but he agreed for my sake to walk out to the end of our *wadi* and no farther.

Not only didn't we see anyone when we ventured out, but we didn't hear anymore voices. We went back to our tent.

John guessed that they had already stopped to camp, and resigned himself to having missed them, when from close by someone called out of the darkness, "Shalom!"

Three young people with backpacks appeared.

*How did we not hear them?* I wondered. *Was it the wind blowing down the wadi that carried away the sound of their footsteps?*

"Sit down; how about some tea?" John immediately offered. I quickly made a mental calculation as to whether we would have enough water for our hike tomorrow.

They explained that they had seen our campfire from the

mountain and wanted to say hello, but planned on hiking farther that night, as they liked walking in the dark.

We found this strange because on the back of all our trail maps under Instructions for Hikers was written: "If you do not reach your target site by nightfall, STOP! Never proceed through unfamiliar terrain in the dark!"

We warned them that the trail would soon take a sharp turn to the left which they would certainly miss at this hour. After exchanging a few words with one another they decided they would gladly take a break and share a cup of tea with us. As fellow hikers, they understood the problem of water and proposed that we use their water if we didn't have enough.

"How about a granola bar with your tea?" John, the perfect host, was offering our choicest delicacy, as if it were the most expensive chocolate we had in our cupboard.

A young woman, Dina, and two young men, Itai and Eli, three friends who often hiked together, had started in Mitzpe Ramon and had planned a three-day trip. Like many young Israelis, they looked as if they hadn't been near a camping store in years, but had just grabbed whatever equipment they had in their house. Some old bulky sleeping bags were tied with string to their beaten-up packs. They told us that a driver who had picked them up hitchhiking had lent them his tent and said they could return it to him later.

We explained that we were on our ninth day of the *Shvil* and were believers in *Yeshua* (Jesus) the Messiah. By this time we were sprawled on the ground around the coals of our fire.

"Unbelievable!" Dina exclaimed.

"What's unbelievable?" John asked.

Dina told us that not wanting to take extra weight, they had decided to take one book between them and read it aloud to each other.

"Okay, so what?" John wanted to know.

Dina was visibly excited as she explained that they had chosen the New Testament, an assignment for her English literature course in university. They were up to chapter eight of the Gospel of Matthew and had many questions. "Maybe you could answer them?" she asked.

I groped behind me in the dark, grabbing some twigs to lay on the glowing embers. The fire flared up again. After living nearly thirty years in Israel, we couldn't remember an encounter with young people who were so eager to hear about *Yeshua*. As we talked in that little *wadi* under the stars in the middle of nowhere, the five of us paused now and then to reflect on this miraculous meeting. John and I were certain that God had ordained our paths to cross in this place.

They were reading the New Testament in English, but we shared with them that it was actually written by Jewish people. Jesus and all His disciples were Jewish and so were the early believers. They seemed to understand as we showed them that the New Testament was a continuation of the Old, and that neither could be understood without the other.

Finally when it was late, they decided to camp a little farther down from us and continue their hike the next day.

"What time do you guys get started in the morning?" Eli asked.

John answered that we were up with the first light and on our way soon after.

"So can you give a knock on our tent as you go? It's hard for us to get up in the morning."

*No wonder they're still hiking in the dark*, I thought.


We knocked on their tent in the morning, but didn't wait for them to wake up. We began hiking, glad we had made the decision not to continue hiking the previous day. The sun rising over the mountains cast a pink glow on the landscape. We also felt pink and fresh and ready to tackle anything. And we wouldn't have wanted to miss our encounter with Dina and her friends.

We battled a powerful wind on the long, steep climb to the top. The air was several degrees colder than it was in the valley and we never would have found a camping spot up there. I was even more thankful for our cozy, relatively warm, *wadi* the night before. As we traversed the barren ridge, I thought this must be like walking on the surface of the moon. The ground was covered with a layer of small sharp stones, and our footsteps made no imprints, and no path could be seen across the bald plateau. The trail signs were hard to find. The *Carbolet*, (which means "cock's comb" or "the crest of a mountain"), jutted into the sky ahead of us, its jagged edge outlined against the sky. Even though I had crossed it once before, I was frightened. *Must be my age*, I thought.

Some sections were indeed like a knife-edge, with sheer drops on both sides, but in other places the narrow path hugged a cliff on one side with a sheer plunge on the other. I trained myself to keep my eyes straight on the trail ahead of me in the same manner that I try to keep my eyes on God and on the path that He has laid out for me. "Let your eyes look straight ahead, fix your gaze directly before you" (Prov. 4:25). I wasn't able to enjoy the sweeping views of the Negev or the fluffy gray cloud formations skittering across the sky.

"Step-by-step," I repeated to myself.

After reaching the highest point, the path went downhill, and I began thinking about Moriah and Jim and our friends from Eilat meeting us in the Bedouin tent in the Ramon Crater. According to my calculations, we had another twelve kilometers to go, perhaps three or four hours walking. After four days in the wilderness, I was surprised at how much I was looking forward to seeing family.

Our lunch break at Ein Saharonim, another Nabatean caravan

stop, was alongside the ruins of the ancient khan or caravanserai. How thankful those camel caravans must have been to reach this spot, the only water source in the Ramon Crater. The ground water level was close to the surface here as evidenced by a dense reed forest growing out of the sand and the smell of water in the air.

In the early afternoon we saw the black Bedouin tent of Be'erot Campground ahead of us, seeming to hover like a dark spaceship on the buff ground. By this time the wind was howling, alternately impelling us forward or pushing us backward. I was grateful we wouldn't be sleeping outside.

Entering the long Bedouin tent, we instantly felt protected and safe from the storm. As our eyes adjusted to the semi-darkness we could see a low wooden table surrounded by colorful pillows and thick, foam mattresses. Rugs covered the floor. At one end of the tent they had arranged a sort of living room with sofas and armchairs in a semi-circle around a stove; and striped, multi-colored, traditional tapestries covered the walls. The pungent smell of the woven goats' hair tent blended with the aromas of roasting coffee and smoke from the fire. The wind rattling the tent sounded like a herd of horses galloping across the roof.

Ahmed, a Bedouin from Rahat, a town near Beer Sheva, managed the campground with the help of a couple of his friends. We had the choice of sleeping outside under a canopy for five dollars or inside the tent for eight dollars. We didn't need a second to decide.

We collapsed on the soft mattresses. John quickly had his boots off and his feet raised. He looked like someone who had just arrived in heaven. While drinking small glasses of sweet Bedouin tea, he began reading his Bible and soon dozed off.

I thought about the three young hikers we had met coming off the *Carbolet*. The one named Yossi, who was a scuba diver, had said he would stay in our hostel when he came to dive in Eilat. We hadn't met many people these ten days, but I was beginning to understand that people were impressed when we told them we were through-hikers on the Israel Trail. Although they didn't say it outright, I think people were surprised that a couple our age would attempt such a trek. And I believe that they also gave us credit for loving the land of Israel, because there is something patriotic about hiking through one's country. Religious Jews liked to remind us that we were fulfilling God's commandment to walk the land. All these situations gave us opportunities to share our faith in Jesus.

At 3 P.M. we heard the sound of a car pulling up, doors slamming, and familiar voices. Moriah, Jim, Julian, Miki, Maxim, and Tomas had driven two hours to join us for a day. After hugs and stories, we spread the food they had brought on the table and reveled in a feast of fresh pita, hummus, vegetables, and fruit. We proposed a drive to Ein Saharonim to explore the Nabatean settlement; it felt strange to be traveling in a car as normal tourists. The dark clouds and strong winds suggested it would start raining any minute. Moriah and Jim brought us the welcome news that things were going well at the Shelter and in the congregation.

In the evening, back in the tent, we all sat around the large wood-burning stove. Two blackened tea kettles and a coffee pot were perched on top, and we grilled our kebabs and hotdogs on the inside rack. The young Bedouin men who managed the campsite and a couple of Israeli guests joined us for talks and music. A man named Ahmed seemed to be thoroughly enjoying himself as he pounded out an incredible rhythm using a traditional carved wooden mortar and pestle, normally used to grind coffee, that he had inherited from his grandfather.

We piled up three mattresses and felt we were lying on clouds.

John roused us early with fresh coffee and tea boiled on the fire pit. The weather had cleared; the herd of wild horses galloped on. After breakfast Jim dropped us off at the trail head and drove up to Mitzpe Ramon with our packs. I felt like skipping and running along the trail without the weight on my back. Having only twelve kilometers to walk, we could take it easy and enjoy the company of Moriah and our friends. Although John and I didn't tire of each other's company, it was nice to talk with someone else for a change. Jim was waiting for us where the trail entered the town, and he drove us to a small restaurant. I savored the sensation of washing my hands with soap before eating, and sitting at a clean table with plates, silverware, and napkins.

Jim brought us to the town's inn after lunch, and our friends returned to Eilat. We took a hot shower, went shopping to replenish our food supply, and luxuriated in relaxing and reading while sprawled out on soft beds with white sheets. To save our fellow guests in the dining room at breakfast from four days of trail aromas, we rinsed our clothes in the shower and dried them over the heater in the bathroom.

"I'm glad we're inside. I hope we don't freeze tomorrow."

"Can you believe we walked to Mitzpe Ramon?"

# 7. A Knife Edge
# & Two Craters

Breakfasted and thoroughly refreshed, we never imagined when we left Mitzpe Ramon the next morning that we would face one of our most challenging days on the Trail: wind, rain, danger of floods, the descent into Nahal Hava, and a cave at the end of the day.

Before falling asleep in the cave, we put our cooking pot outside to catch water for tea the next morning. We dozed off to the plunk, plunk of dripping rain.

The first thing we did the next morning was to check on the rain and the water level in the *wadi*. Would we be able to leave our cave, or would we be trapped? We thanked God that, though the day was cold and cloudy and there were pools in the streambed, the rain had stopped and the wind had abated.

I was prepared for a strenuous day because Sde Boker, our destination, was at least a twenty-kilometer hike. We would experience three oases, including Ein Zik, where we had first conceived the idea to walk the Trail.

Stepping over the crest of the hill we spied those familiar palm and poplar trees of Ein Zik again.

"Take a picture, Jupe," John said. "It's exactly a year since we met Uri and his girlfriend here. Can you believe we did it, that we're actually on the *Shvil*?"

"Yeah, let's stop for lunch." I was feeling nostalgic.

We sat on rocks in the damp shade of the poplars, but with a long trip ahead, we couldn't rest for long.

The next oasis, Upper Ein Akev, was virgin territory for us. I always walk with an extra bounce in my step when visiting a new place, and it's exciting to see water and palm trees in the middle of the wilderness. Upper Ein Akev, carved deeply between two cliffs, is a meandering stream bordered by lush vegetation. As we crossed the *wadi* back and forth, we found ourselves alternately laughing and complaining as we slipped and slid on the slippery faces of the rocks. The singing wind, rippling the reeds and fluttering the leaves of the tamarisk trees, was a pleasant change from the strong, unrestrained gusts we were used to.

Then, as abruptly as it had started, the vegetation was gone, and we continued up the dry streambed until we came to the top of a ten-meter waterfall—Lower Ein Akev springs.

We didn't linger in any of these places because I was eager to get to the field school in Sde Boker before the office closed. As usual, my mind was racing ahead, and according to my calculations it would take us six days to get from Sde Boker to the town of Arad on the border of the Judean Desert and the Negev. We needed to get advice at the field school because there were no settlements in between and we couldn't carry that many provisions.

The Israel Trail headed down toward the waterfall's base, but since we needed to stock up on water and food, we made a long detour to the closest store. Hiking along a ridge, and passing Bedouin tents, we finally saw the settlement of Sde Boker.

"Almost there now, Jupe!" John announced. "We'll definitely make it before the office closes at four."

I still had my doubts. Wasn't Sde Boker perched above Nahal Zin, a broad *wadi*? Maybe we weren't as close as we thought.

It looked as if we could throw a stone over into the village; we were at the same elevation. But another five minutes of walking revealed an enormous gap between us and our goal. We arrived an hour later after a knee-aching descent and heart-pounding ascent on the other side.

Sde Boker, the *kibbutz* as well as the college, is associated with David Ben Gurion, Israel's first prime minister, who had an almost mystical connection with the desert. When the borders of Israel were being debated in 1947 and 1948, Ben Gurion was convinced the modern nation should include the Negev, though at the time it was virtually uninhabited and thought to be uncultivable. Nevertheless, he believed this region was needed in order for Israel to grow; he saw it as a place where the people could settle and prosper. It was not just a theoretical conviction for Ben Gurion, because in 1953 he joined the new *kibbutz* of Sde Boker and lived there after he retired from politics, sharing in the endeavor to tame the desert. Wine grapes are the *kibbutz*'s main crop today, and their packaging tape factory is a major source of income.

Ben Gurion and his wife, Paula, are buried next to the Sde Boker College.

At 3:30 A.M., delighted to arrive at the Field School, I dashed by the receptionist at the hostel and went straight to the guide room. It was my kind of place, with maps hanging on all the walls and the young guides enthusiastically discussing trips. After examining the appropriate map and conferring with one of the guides about the nature of the trails and the terrain ahead of us, we concluded that we would hike two days over the *Carbolet* to the Oron phosphate factory. From there we would hitchhike to Arad for the weekend to stay with friends and attend their congregation.

I feared the *Carbolet* more than any Trail segment and looked forward to have a weekend to recover after traversing it. Under the heading, "Level of Difficulty," my *Israel Trail* book ranked this portion as "a difficult route, for experienced hikers only." My heart palpitated even opening that page. After Arad we would return to where we left off, with a four day journey before reaching the more inhabited sections of the Trail. This seemed a more reasonable approach than packing food for six days.

While I was poring over the maps, John was chatting with the receptionist whom he recognized from his previous visit to Sde Boker.

"What happened to you?!" she asked. "You look like you blew in from the North Pole!"

"We're on the *Shvil Israel*," John answered. "It's been a long day. Slept last night in a cave. Would you have a room for us here? When you're in Eilat, you can stay at the Shelter."

*Does he have to say that to absolutely everyone?* I thought. For some reason this woman didn't look like the type who'd be interested in hiking or staying in a hostel. To my surprise, however, she seemed to be genuinely considering John's offer.

We checked into the hostel, and after a hot shower we went shopping in the small grocery store and enjoyed a warm meal in the cafeteria. We had all our warm clothes on: fleeces, wind jackets, gloves, and hats, and were still freezing. I couldn't believe we would normally be sleeping outside in this weather. The forecast was for the cold spell to continue. When would it end and average temperatures return?

I wrote in my diary:

- *When we know we're going to a warm place, the travel is easier.*
- *Good company on the trail is important.*
- *Most of the trail is up or down with occasional flat stretches.*

As a metaphor of life, the trail continued to teach me. The anticipation of a comfortable rest at the end of the day is like my assurance that when I die I have a place prepared for me in heaven, because of my faith in the Lord Jesus. This hope permeates all my life, because I know that trials, suffering, and disappointments are only temporary and a far better place awaits me. Furthermore, I learned that faithful, compatible company on the trail is essential just as it is in our daily lives.

When we stepped out of our room in the morning we noticed a silvery shine on the windshields of cars. Upon closer examination we were astonished to see frost; we were glad we had slept inside.

We needed to link up with the Israel Trail again. John, having explored this area before, calculated that we could take a short-cut down the side of the cliff into the *wadi* and then cut across to the jeep trail. For me, it was the first time I had hiked in the 120 kilometer-long Nahal Zin, the Negev's second longest *wadi*. When Moses sent out spies to scout the Promised Land, they passed through Nahal Zin, and I imagined us following in their footsteps.

Down in the *wadi* with its many dips and rises, we couldn't see our route. I took out the map when we reached a red jeep trail, but didn't see the corresponding stripe on the chart. I like maps and enjoy figuring out where we're going, whether on a car journey or on a hike. I'm not an expert navigator, however, and I began to doubt myself, especially when I saw another red line on the map going off in a different direction.

"Something's wrong here," I said. "Now I'm really confused. I didn't feel right from the beginning about taking that short-cut."

"Come on Jupe, don't you think I know where we are?" John was becoming upset with me. "You know I've been here lots of times."

I was becoming more and more disoriented and nervous.

"Okay, don't you trust me then?"

I prayed to keep calm and asked God to help us find the way.

"You know I trust you."

"Do you want to follow the markings and walk extra kilometers?" John asked. "The map's wrong."

I looked at the map and saw it was issued in 2001. Perhaps they had added a new trail since then.

In the midst of my discouragement we suddenly merged into another trail. I could tell it was the right one because the blue slashes painted on the rocks went in the same direction as the blue stripe on our map. I thanked God and felt relaxed again, glad that most of the time John and I used our differences to balance each other, not to quarrel.

We cheerfully trekked through the desolate Nahal Zin, meeting no people, no jeeps, no acacia trees, not even many shrubs.

The trail turned and began to head toward the mountain range to the north. We knew that eventually we would be climbing up a *wadi* there to the *Carbolet*, so we assumed we were getting closer to our destination. We ate lunch in a flower-filled *wadi*, but were too cold to sit for long. Suddenly the trail curved onto a jeep road heading away from the mountains. We walked a few minutes thinking we would soon turn back, but the Israel Trail signs kept leading us away.

John was bothered and mumbled, "Looks like we're heading back to Eilat."

"Now don't get upset, they must know what they're doing," I said, acting superior in my turn. We were following the signs, and as long as I could see the markers, I didn't worry.

"I'm not upset, but this is nonsense. Why did they do this to us?" John had lost all faith in the planners of the trail.

"Just calm down," I urged him. "At least we're not lost, right?"

Our route finally circled back to the mountains and about two hours after lunch we came to a trail that looked as if it would have taken us here from our lunch spot in half an hour. Why indeed did they do that to us?

We headed into a narrow, white sandstone canyon, noticeably a place where others had camped. This was either the last suitable camping site before ascending the *Carbolet* or the first place to camp after coming off it. Observing a few footprints and scattered fire pits, I was comforted to see that people had made it safely across the dreaded knife edge.

I had become concerned when a friend who was also interested in the *Shvil* had told me the *Carbolet* could only be traveled from north to south—the opposite direction than we were going. But when I mentioned this on the phone with Danny, the Israel Trail coordinator, he told me it wasn't true; he had led a group of pensioners across. Whom should I believe? Danny was certainly more knowledgeable, but the seeds of doubt had been planted in my mind. I tried to think logically and tell myself that I didn't need to be scared. We read the newspaper regularly, and I couldn't remember anything about people breaking their necks falling off the *Carbolet*. Surely such an accident would warrant mention in the news. So if others had made it over safely, why wouldn't I?

It was our tenth night of camping. I loved the beauty of the place, the simple routine. As John built a fire I wrote in my diary:

- *Trust John.*
- *Trust God.*
- *It will all work out.*
- *Don't worry.*

The next morning we woke up early as usual. We gained elevation quickly as we hiked. From our campsite I could see a slope with gigantic boulders above us. On the map it was labeled "seasonal pools." From my experience I felt sure that the trail would lead us around the house-sized rocks, via switchbacks along the side; to our surprise, however, we headed straight toward the rock fall.

We were in Nahal Ofran, a *wadi* I had never heard of. No one had warned me about it, perhaps because most people hike down it instead of up, although that would also be tricky. Later when we met a group of hikers and began speaking about the *Carbolet*, they asked if we had hiked up Nahal Ofran. When I said that I wasn't sure of the name of the *wadi*, they asked, "Was it insane?"

"Definitely!" I replied.

"Then that was Nahal Ofran."

We were climbing up, around, and under the enormous stones. Trying to keep our bodies close to the rock face, we pulled ourselves up smooth surfaces at seventy-five-degree angles. There were few handholds; John went up first and reached down for me to grasp his hand. In some impossible spots, the Trails Authority had anchored metal clamps into the stone. At that, I started laughing.

"I can't believe we're doing this, at our age!"

We crawled on a narrow ledge over a deep chasm and hauled ourselves slowly up the nearly vertical slab on the other side.

John tried to keep up a pleasant banter, hoping to encourage me. "If you fall in here," John said, looking down, "you'd have a hard time getting out."

"Thanks, don't tell me about it," I replied, trying to ignore the obvious danger.

The ascent seemed to go on and on. Each time we thought we were on top, the path took another turn, and there was another *wadi*, another *gev*. After two and a half hours, we reached a crest. We got good reception on our phone, so we made some calls and ate a granola bar. Racheli told us she was worried because snow was forecast in our area.

We recognized from our high position that the *Carbolet* wasn't a simple knife-edge along the rim of one mountain. Rather, there were many ups and downs into different *wadi*s. Perhaps for this reason "cock's comb," the literal translation of *carbolet*, most accurately describes the ridge.

The *Carbolet* constitutes the southeastern rim of the Maktesh Hagadol, or Large Crater. There are three craters in Israel: the Ramon, the Large, and the Small. While the Ramon Crater is shaped like an elongated heart and has one undefined edge, the Large, or Maktesh, Crater is shaped like an enormous footstep squished into the mud, ten kilometers long and four wide. *Maktesh* is Hebrew for "mortar," as in mortar and pestle. Unlike impact craters caused by meteorites, these erosion craters are a geological phenomenon unique to Israel. In fact, the word *maktesh* has been introduced into the world's scientific literature meaning "eroded valley."

Large sections of the trail are truly like walking on the blade of a thick knife. On our left the cut-away mountain dropped straight down into the Large Crater, and our right side slid down like a steep roof. Walking with our left leg a step higher than the right demanded constant concentration. Our poles provided balance, and thankfully the rough rock face supplied adequate footholds. Although John sometimes strode right along the edge, I found that I didn't have to march precisely on the brim but could cut across a few meters below it. As usual I was grateful to find that my anxiety had been unjustified.

To our right we had a fabulous view of Nahal Zin and could see the oasis of Ein Zik with its palm trees—a green nugget in the sunburned wilderness. It was hard to believe we had passed by there two days earlier. Up ahead of us was the Oron Phosphate Factory, a huge eyesore in the pristine landscape.

After hours on the cock's comb, we came to a steep incline and picked our way rock by rock down a jagged face. By this time our legs wobbled and our bodies were exhausted. The *Shvil* intersected an access road to the factory. I had read in the Israel Trail book that many people detour from here to the main gate of the plant to refill their water bottles. With the sun already low over the horizon, we knew we could never complete the last four kilometers of the *Carbolet* before darkness fell.

"It's been enough," said John.

I agreed. "We've been on the trail for nine days without a day off. We can hitch to our friends in Arad."

When we found the factory gate, we felt like weary soldiers coming off the battlefield. Mahmoud, a friendly Bedouin guard, showed us the water faucet. We were trudging out to the main road to Yeroham, a small town nearby, when Mahmoud came by in his pickup and drove us to the junction.

An Israeli couple who were part of a group of four jeeps making a trip in the Negev stopped for us, explaining they had changed their route because of the poor weather. We joined their tour, and they drove us to an overlook from where we could see a large portion of our day's trail. They were impressed as we pointed out all the crags and dips in our route.

They dropped us off, and we waited an hour until a man named Rami stopped for us. He told us his life's story, which sounded like a movie script. After divorcing his wife in Israel he had traveled to Thailand, where he met a young Thai woman and moved in with her. Although they had no common language, they loved each other. He also loved Thailand and lived like a king, he said, though it wasn't clear to us what he had been doing there. Eventually he was homesick and came back to Israel, leaving his beloved in Thailand.

Rami brought us to the bus station in Beer Sheva where we found a shared taxi to the town of Arad. We shivered as we waited for our friend Yakim to pick us up and take us to his home. We had made it—across the *Carbolet* and most of the way through the Negev—to a warm house, a delicious meal, and soft beds.

The trail seemed far off. "I'm glad we're here," I said.


We awoke in Arad to pouring rain. I was thankful we weren't

drenched on the *Carbolet*—I could imagine myself slipping and falling off the cliff, or sliding down the rock face on the other side. We heard on the radio that a severe cold front had gripped the country, but that rising temperatures were forecast.

In the morning we went to the small Hebrew-speaking Messianic congregation, one of the fellowships of Israelis who believe in *Yeshua* that thrive in most towns in Israel. I melted in my chair when the singing began, experiencing the warmth and refreshment of worship with other believers. In the evening we participated in a Russian-speaking group. Since the massive Russian immigration that began with the fall of the Iron Curtain, over a million Russian Jews have come to Israel, and many have started to believe as we do.

Our friend Steve drove down from his *moshav* (cooperative village) in Galilee to meet us Saturday evening. He was hiking the Trail section by section, over a period of a couple of years, and offered to drive us back to where we had left off at the Oron Factory. Staying with a family, we couldn't start early as we were used to. We fit ourselves into their schedule, eating breakfast with them before the children went to school. It was fun to share in the morning time around the table; it reminded me of the days when our children were young.

By the time we arrived at Ein Yorkeam, our starting point, it was 9 A.M. Two young men, Ran and Asaf, were packing up their tent next to the parking lot; they told us they were on a two-and-a-half month trek through the Negev, begun the day they had finished their army service. They filtered water from *gevim* (cisterns) and springs, and were surviving mainly on rice with a few spices they had brought from home.

We had planned for Steve to walk with us a while, return to his car, then drive ahead to meet us at the end of the day.

"We'll watch your car for you if you want," Ran offered. "We're waiting for friends."

"Why watch the car? What's the problem?" John asked.

"Didn't you see the glass in the parking lot? Bedouins on the lookout for cars left by hikers break in and steal everything, if they don't make off with the car too," Asaf explained.

After such a positive encounter with Mahmoud two days earlier, we were sad to hear that unscrupulous locals were taking advantage of people who simply wanted to enjoy nature. Thankful for their offer of help, Steve agreed to be back in an hour and then drive the two young men up the road to their trail head.

At Ein Yorkeam, where a spring flows in a rocky canyon, carved steps led from a small Nabatean fort down to the edge of the green-tinted water. Farther on, with the help of an iron ladder bolted into the cliff, we descended into the spectacular Nahal Hatira, a banquet for our eyes with its purple, yellow and white flowers, green grass, majestic acacias, and Atlantic oaks.

Following a steep climb out of the *wadi* and a tramp through desolate country, we arrived at the place we'd planned to meet Steve, a campground above the Small Crater. Without packs, we hiked faster than we had expected, and since it was only 2 P.M., Steve suggested we continue to the next camping spot near the mouth of the crater. He spread carpets on the ground and prepared a refreshing cup of tea on his primus stove. Soon we were on our way again, hoping to arrive before dark.

I was nervous; hiking with jeep support is an entirely different approach to the *Shvil*. We eliminated the weight of backpacks, but depended on arranged meeting points where the jeep had access to the Trail. Without our sleeping bags, tent, and food on our backs, we weren't free to stop wherever we wanted.

Of Israel's three craters, the circular Maktesh Hakatan, or Small Crater, looks the most obviously like a mortar bowl in which a pestle grinds out grain. When viewed from the rim in the late afternoon, the long shadows accentuated the gullies flowing toward the crater's mouth, like veins in a round leaf. Once down inside the crater, we were back at sea level, and after weeks of cold weather were enveloped by balmy, windless air. The broad trail through the crater was easy as a sidewalk. With no backpack, I imagined I was on one of my evening power-walks around Eilat.

We made good time and reached the campground on the other side of the Small Crater as the sun was setting. Located not far from the Dead Sea and near another phosphate factory, it was an unappealing site, barren and exposed. These factories, though they are important to our economy, didn't contribute to the natural landscape.

The Negev Desert and the Dead Sea contain rich reserves of minerals: potash, magnesium, phosphate, and others, that together with local expertise are the basis of a developed chemical industry in Israel. Most products are exported, bringing billions of dollars into Israel every year.

I looked around and fear gripped me. A sign said "camping" and the remains of campfires left no doubt we were in the right place, but where was Steve?

I tried not to think about spending the night with no sleeping bags or tent. Hiking without packs was easier, but I decided I preferred the security of having all my supplies on my back.

"He should have been here by now. I'll give him a call." John, usually cool, sounded concerned.

John switched on his phone, but in this isolated location had no reception.

Steve had come all the way here to help us and maybe something terrible had happened to him.

"Let's pray," John reminded me. "God, you know exactly where Steve is. Protect him on his way and we pray we'll find each other before it gets too dark."

Having no choice, we waited, and in five minutes our ears picked up the distant sound of a car engine.

"Sorry," said Steve stepping out of his jeep. "It's hard to

believe down here in the desert, but I got held up in a traffic jam with dozens of buses outside Dimona." Israel's nuclear facility near the small town of Dimona employs hundreds of workers.

Steve erected his tent next to ours. Two tents instead of one; we had the cozy feeling of being part of a group that night. He produced all kinds of fancy camping gear from his jeep: a flashlight, grill, ice chest, and rug.

Rose, Steve's wife, had prepared a feast for us—chicken seasoned with herbs, homemade bread, beans, baked potatoes, chocolate cookies, fresh milk for the coffee and more—the best meal we had eaten on the Trail.

Breakfast the next morning was also a dramatic change from our usual pita with peanut butter and an apple. Weetabix™ with milk (Steve is British), fresh rolls, cheese, yogurt, and fruit gave us a five-star launch for the day.

Then, hiking back into the crater to the *Shvil* cutoff, we noticed evidence of a flood that had surged through the narrow canyon a few months before. The torrent had swept away part of the road and had lodged branches in the tops of the electric poles—an incredible display of nature's power.

The arduous climb out of the Small Crater rewarded us with breathtaking views and an abundance of flowers.

"Jupe, take a picture!"

We were gazing over the Arava Valley at the mountains of Moab in Jordan.

"Do you see that white streak hanging over the horizon?" John pointed with his walking stick.

"Yeah, looks cloudy over there."

"Can't you see? It's snow!" The Jordanian mountains, higher than Israel's, receive occasional snowfalls, a beautiful sight, and a result of the exceptional cold snap.

"Let me look at the camera. Can you see the snow in the photo?" John was excited as a child.

Up on the ridge, we began to see camels for the first time, a sign we were entering a populated area. Their slow movements as they grazed among the thorny bushes caught our eye, although their brown, cream, tan, and even white colors blended in with the desert background. Many people think the camels they see grazing alone are wild. All of the camels in the Negev, however, belong to Bedouins. The average price for a camel in Israel is $2,000, while the prized white one fetches three or four times that amount.

With its distinctive hump, long, thin legs and knobby knees, large mouth and wide nostrils, doe-like eyes, curly eyelashes and bushy eyebrows, you want to laugh just looking at the camel. Though an odd-looking creature, it is perfectly suited to its environment. The hump, often misunderstood as a place for water storage, is a mound of fatty tissue from which the camel draws sustenance when food is scarce. A camel is able to lose a quarter of its body weight without impairing its normal functions; it can live up to fifty days without water in the winter, and five days in the summer. A thirsty camel can drink as much as eighty liters of water in one session. In the Sinai we saw Bedouins "tanking up" their camels before a trip by pouring bucket after bucket into their pried-open mouths.

After descending into Nahal Tsafit, one of the dramatic streambeds in the area, we came to a place where two trails crossed. Noticing on the map that a short side trip up the *wadi* would bring us to Ein Tsafit, a desert spring, we plunked down our packs and scrambled up the rocks. Water trickled down rocky chutes and accumulated in depressions. When the ground finally leveled out, we were treated to a stunning scene—a clear azure sky above craggy brown cliffs, towering over shallow pools of aquamarine water lying in smooth white sandstone. No trees grew around Ein Tsafit; the canyon was too narrow.

Our topographical maps provide information about such things as hiking and jeep trails, animal footprints, and plants and trees of the region. On the map we were using, under the heading springs and water holes, I read that the water from Ein Tsafit flows year-round and is potable. So brushing aside the little creatures swimming on the surface, John filled up an empty water bottle.

"Just in case," I agreed.

"Jupe, take a picture."

Out of the mountains, we crossed the highway to Eilat and entered a totally different landscape. The dramatic view of the desert changed into a jeep track meandering through rolling hills, a pleasant variation. The greenish tint of the land in the distance proved on closer approach to be fine blades of grass sprouting from between the rocks, along with a dark green succulent plant spreading like groundcover. Purple and yellow flowers contributed a burst of color to the beige terrain. Herds of camels and sheep along with their Bedouin shepherds gave us the feeling we had been transported in a time machine back to Bible times.

Though we were now free from the peril of edges and ledges, a new menace arose: dogs. Every Bedouin encampment possessed semi-wild guard dogs. They would begin yapping like crazy as we approached, baring their teeth and rushing straight toward us. John, my protector, walked on the side of the trail nearest the dogs. They always backed off eventually; and after a couple of incidents John learned that when he bent over to pick up a stone, the dogs quickly fled.

We had developed a rapid, easy rhythm, when suddenly we noticed movement in the far distance.

"Hey, look," John said. "Two guys on motorcycles."

I strained to see them. "Yeah, they're coming this way fast, but I don't see any motorcycle dust."

In a few minutes two young men with big backpacks and poles like ours came into sight over a rise. Were we walking so slowly that they seemed to be on motorcycles?

The young men introduced themselves as Yaron and Mor, university students who were walking a section of the Trail for a week between semesters.

"Wow, let's take a picture," Yaron said. "This is the first time we've met two other people with walking sticks."

"Those packs look heavy," John said. "How much weight are you carrying?"

"Not much, just nineteen kilos."

John and I looked at each other. *Just* nineteen kilos? John's eighteen kilos were killing him.

They asked about the new *Shvil* sections, explaining they had mistakenly left this particular map at home. Since we were entering the territory of the next map, I gave them the one they needed, thankful to have fewer grams to carry. We gave them a tract and invited them to visit the Shelter.

By 4:30 P.M. I was ready to stop, but there weren't any decent camping places nearby. Having seen several Bedouin pickup trucks and a couple of army jeeps, we felt that it was important to be in a hidden place. Doubtless we had no reason to worry. The soldiers were here to protect us and the Bedouin are generally peaceful, but we were unexpectedly aware of our vulnerability as two lone campers.

We had felt secure up to this time camping in the wilderness, but we didn't want to take chances if there were people around. I wondered how it would be after we passed Arad and the trails stretch close to the Green Line, which is the border between Israel and the Palestinian territories. Would it be safe to camp in a place where there were terrorist incursions? I knew God would take care of us; for now I just needed to rest and eat.

Finally we noticed a little canyon next to the road, with a beautiful broom tree growing under a cliff.

"Perfect!" John exclaimed. "What could be better than

sleeping under a broom tree? Take a picture, Jupe!"

I was happy to sleep anywhere after ten hours hiking, but I understood John's excitement. The Bible prophet Elijah's great victory on Mt. Carmel over the 450 prophets of Baal and the 400 prophets of Asherah, completely exhausted him. When the wicked Queen Jezebel threatened to kill him, the Bible says, "Elijah was afraid and ran for his life." From Beersheba he went a days' journey into the desert, "came to a broom tree, sat down under it and prayed that he might die ... then he lay down under the tree and fell asleep" (1 Ki. 19:3-6). Through sleep and a pita provided by an angel, Elijah was strengthened and able to go on.

Under our broom tree we prepared a dinner of tuna and Szechwan noodles. We heard sheep bleating as they passed on the road overhead, but felt protected, concealed under our tree next to the cliff. We leaned comfortably against the rocks around our tiny fire, an energy bar and an apple completing our feast. Here on the edge of the Judean Desert, we could feel warmth in the air.

God willing, we would be in Arad tomorrow evening, staying with Yakim and his family again, with the desert, the most difficult part of the Trail, completed. One of my fears before starting this trip had been the cold, but thank God, He had helped us so far.


The next day started easily, on a flat jeep trail. According to the map we would be on a jeep trail most of the way to Arad, so we expected to make good time. In general, walking along a jeep trail is easier than walking on a hiking path. A vehicle requires a wider, smoother and more moderately-graded route than do hikers. But soon we started to climb. The road was steep, rocky, and the wind was against us; not at all what we had expected.

"This is nonsense!" John grumbled. "It could take us two days to reach Arad at this rate."

Finally we reached the summit of Mt. Yahel, a 400-meter

climb. After an hour on a flat path, we were opposite Arad. The Israel Trail veered off to the east, but a short-cut led into town.

"It's only 12:30 p.m. and we don't have to get to Yakim's so early," John suggested.

"Yeah," I agreed, "looks like it would only be an extra three kilometers or so to stay on the *Shvil*." I hated to miss any of the Trail and we would still arrive in Arad in the early afternoon.

We decided to stay on the trail and found ourselves heading away from town and going down towards the Dead Sea. I could tell that John wasn't happy.

"I'm not angry," he insisted. "But this just doesn't make sense to me. We're going exactly the opposite direction than we should. The Trail planners made a huge mistake here."

I had to agree we were getting farther and farther away from Arad, our destination. Instead of north into Arad, we were heading due east towards the Dead Sea.

"But look, we're following the Trail signs." I tried to remain positive, though I too was bothered as we lost the altitude we had gained with such effort that morning.

Just when John was certain we would soon be swimming in the Dead Sea, the Trail turned sharply and dipped into Nahal Ye'elim, which had once been a lovely *wadi*. Now, unfortunately close to the road from Arad to the Dead Sea, in some spots it looked like a trash dump. After hiking through clean unspoiled country, the garbage bothered us. The refuse included wrecks of cars that had missed the turns in the curvy road and plunged into the abyss.

"If this crazy detour took us through a beautiful *wadi* I could understand it," John said. "But to walk all this extra way through this junk, who needs it?"

As we slowly negotiated enormous boulders, John was becoming more and more agitated. "When's this going to end?" he muttered. "We were nearly in Arad three hours ago."

At last the *Shvil* emerged from the *wadi* and trail markers on

lampposts led us to the commercial center of Arad. The time was
4 P.M. We collapsed on a city bench in the town square. Falafel
stands, kiosks, newsstands, gift shops, and mini-markets lined the
street; shoppers strolled up and down.

"Got a few shekels? I'll get us something to drink," I told
John, and walked over to pick up two cokes.

"I called Yakim," John told me when I returned. "He's on his
way to get us. Can you believe we walked from Eilat to Arad?"

"Yeah, we've never done that before."

Eighteen days through the wilderness. When preparing for
the trip I wasn't able to project any farther than Arad, the
symbolic division between the southern desert and the northern,
more inhabited part of the Trail. For the rest of the trip we had
plenty of friends along the way who would be willing to help
us if necessary by picking us up, bringing us food, or letting us
stay with them. I had a list of names and phone numbers that
John carried in his pouch. We would be crossing roads every day
and walking close to settlements—*kibbutzim*, *moshavim*, cities, and
Arab towns—where we could stock up on food and water. I had
sent four maps covering the center of Israel to Yakim, so that night
I would try to plan our journey from there. I had a feeling it would
be a different kind of adventure.

In the meantime we had learned a lot. Our bodies were
stronger. We had seen some amazing places in Israel that we never
knew existed. We still loved each other, and had successfully
overcome our differences.

Yakim pulled up with three of his children in the car. "Here,
let me help you with those packs," he said.

# 8. Lightening the Load

At Yakim and Debbie's home, we collapsed on the soft sofa and savored the comfortable feeling of being inside and out of the wind.

The children enjoyed hearing stories about our journey and receiving the presents I'd brought them. I normally love scouring the ground to collect interesting rocks and fossils on our hikes, but on the *Shvil* I restrained myself from adding extra weight. Knowing, however, that I could unload my treasures with Yakim's children, I brought them a few crystals I discovered that day.

"I'm sorry," Yakim informed us soon after our arrival, "but we had planned to go meet some other friends. You're welcome to come, but we'll understand if you'd rather stay here."

We preferred to stay in their home and rest. After a delicious shower we began unpacking and spreading our stuff all over their living room. What a blessing to have friends who made us feel so welcome. John had been frustrated in the afternoon when he felt we were walking in a loop, going kilometers out of the way. Once we reached Arad, however, all was forgotten and we were both in top spirits.

"Listen," John proposed. "Here's what I was thinking: we'll leave our sleeping bags, tent, and ground pads here, and from now on we'll sleep at people's houses." Up till now, I had envisioned sleeping out every night, except occasionally when we were near a friend's house.

"What!?" I couldn't quite grasp what he meant.

"These packs are heavy. Coming up to Arad today was a killer. And we're not so young anymore either, you know."

After twenty-nine years of marriage, I thought I knew John well. But this time he really surprised me. Looking back, I suppose I could have guessed he was ready for a change when he kept insisting earlier that day that he "definitely wasn't upset" while struggling up the frustrating Nahal Ye'elim.

Of course we weren't so young; that was obvious. And certainly this had been a rough day—not just physically, but mentally, too. At noon we had been in sight of Arad, but then began following the Israel Trail signs towards the Dead Sea. After that we hiked up Nahal Ye'elim, one of the most unattractive and trash-filled *wadis* I had seen in my life. And it was a steep climb; our packs had weighed heavily on our backs. We had lost the Trail signs a number of times and hiked out of our way.

But was John going to give up sleeping out in our cozy little tent, cooking our Thai rice or Indian curry on the campfire, and eating our pita and peanut butter for breakfast? I had become attached to our routine and to the simplicity of life on the Trail.

"Where will we sleep?"

"Every evening we'll simply make sure we get to a road, and then we'll hitch to wherever we're going." John reminded me of the list I had made of our friends. I could tell he was settled on this new arrangement.

I couldn't believe that the morning under the broom tree was the last time we would wake up to the expansive views of nature. It sounded like an awful lot of coming and going on roads to me. John seemed to enjoy the hitchhiking—I think it made him feel young again. But I found it annoying.

Nevertheless, I couldn't deny that we'd still be hiking the

Israel Trail. We would still cover the entire course, and had anyone made a rule about the *Shvil* that you had to sleep out every night? I knew there were endless approaches to it.

John knew how I felt, but I'd learned that some things are not worth quarrelling about. Furthermore, while it's often possible to compromise, here we either had to carry the camping gear we needed to sleep outside, or travel lighter and stay with friends.

"Don't forget," John said, "till now we've been in the desert, but from here on we'll be close to civilization." He didn't like the idea of camping where people might see us, especially in the sections close to the Green Line, the border between Israel and the Palestinian Authority.

"Tomorrow we'll be less than fifteen kilometers from Hebron," he added. Hebron, one of the larger Palestinian cities, is one of the places of the greatest unrest.

I couldn't argue. Just a few weeks previously a terrorist had snuck over the border and stabbed a security guard at Bet Guvrin, a national park a few days farther along our route. We frequently heard on the news about drive-by shootings and even attacks on hikers. While committed to hiking the *Shvil*, I didn't want to act irresponsibly, especially when I thought about our four children. I had learned through the years to trust John, and was confident in his gift of weighing the options and making the right decision.

When Yakim and Debbie came home we shared with them our new method for hiking the Trail. They didn't mind keeping our gear, which filled two large garbage bags, until one of our friends could bring it to Eilat. Debbie suggested that we call Yakim's parents in the small town of Omer, and perhaps we could sleep at their house the following night.

Yakim's mother, Hanna, told us on the phone that she would be delighted to host us, and I began to feel more optimistic about John's strategy to lighten our load.

* * *

Our stomachs were full and our packs lighter when we left the house the next morning. We were beginning a new adventure, and I sincerely hoped we'd enjoy hiking the Trail this way.

The spring-like weather, with a warm sun beginning to burn through the early morning haze, contrasted sharply with the previous rainy *shabbat* (Saturday, Israel's day of rest) we had spent in Arad.

After breakfast, Yakim drove us to the edge of town where we picked up the *Shvil* again. Yesterday we had hiked through the Judean Desert—an arid, brown, rocky landscape with only a greenish tint of short grass. Now we walked through emerald wheat fields. From the outskirts of Arad, Tel Arad stuck out of the flat cropland like a miniature volcano. (A *tel* is a mound formed when successive civilizations build their city on the ruins of previous settlements.)

As we walked through flat agricultural lands, we noticed trail markers knocked to the side by tractors; or lifted out of place by streaming *wadis* after a rainfall. The signs frequently pointed in the wrong direction, misleading us. But we kept our sights on the *tel*, knowing that the *Shvil* passed alongside it.

The town of Arad was continuously settled through the years due to its strategic location. As early as 3000 B.C., trading expeditions passed by bringing copper from Timna and the Sinai, and bitumen (asphalt) from the Dead Sea.

The Bible says that near the end of the Israelites' desert wanderings, the Canaanite king of Arad heard that Israel was approaching, ordered an attack, and seized captives. Israel went on to destroy Arad, later converting it into an important fortress to protect Israel's southeast border from the Amalekites and the Edomites, two nations of nomadic invaders and Israel's chief enemies. Archaeologists have uncovered the remains of an Israelite temple, a remarkable discovery since worship centers outside Jerusalem were forbidden in the Law of Moses.

We climbed Har Amasa, one of the higher hills in the area, situated on the ruins of an old Roman road. The timeworn thoroughfare, its ancient cobblestones set in rows with piled rocks defining the sides, provided a relatively smooth trail for us. I pictured Roman soldiers marching over the roadbed on their way from Jerusalem to Edom or Eilat, and chariots rumbling over these same paving stones.

On top of the cold, gusty ridge we met Mohammed, a Bedouin shepherd. Although the Bedouin language is Arabic, most men speak some Hebrew. After greeting one another, he told us he had lost his cell phone up here two days ago.

"What's your number?" John asked. "I'll call it for you."

I didn't want to sound pessimistic, but it seemed to me the phone could be hidden under any puny bush or next to any of the thousands of rocks. Shouting to make ourselves heard above the howling wind, what chance did we have of hearing the ring? Nevertheless, our new acquaintance appreciated John's offer and was delighted when, having asked for some water, John gave him a full bottle as well as four *pitot* (the term used for more than one pita) and a few oranges. I was pleased with lighter packs, and happy to share our water with a lonely shepherd. Once when we had been low on water on our way to Arad, we encountered two Bedouin shepherd girls. We motioned with our hands and stuttered over our few words of Arabic to communicate our request for water. They gladly complied; one of the girls filled our bottle from the large jerry-can she carried on her back.

We waved good-bye to Mohammed and continued on to the Amasa summit. The overlook provided a view of the whole area: from the Judean Desert and the mountains of Moab to the Yatir Forest, our next objective. We passed a group of older tour guides on a retraining course who recognized from our hiking sticks and our large, dirty backpacks that we were dedicated hikers.

"Where're you from?" one asked.

"We're on the *Shvil Israel,*" answered John. "We started in Eilat nineteen days ago and are on our way to Kibbutz Dan."

Impressed, one after another stopped to ask us questions. "Well done!" they declared.

"Here," John offered, "you can read about our trip in this pamphlet we wrote."

Farther along we met a smartly-dressed young religious couple. They introduced themselves as Barak and Abigail, from a nearby settlement, and said they were enjoying a short walk. We knew they were religious Jews by the *kippa* (skullcap) on his head and by her long dress, long sleeves, and head scarf.

"Would you mind taking a picture with us?" Barak asked, after we explained we were hiking the Israel Trail.

In Israel the various branches of religious Jews are distinguished by their clothing and head coverings. The men who are Orthodox but not as ardent as others will simply have a *kippa* or *yarmulke* on their heads, a black one for the more stringent sects and an embroidered one for the less so.

The ultra-Orthodox branches separate themselves further from society both in dress and lifestyle. Their men wear black clothes and black hats, and have long beards and side curls. Followers live together in their own neighborhoods and spend their days studying in a *yeshiva* (an academy for the study of Jewish texts).

Few of the "black-coats" live in Eilat; it's too hot, and besides, our city has a reputation for vice and immorality, a sort of Israeli version of Miami Beach or Las Vegas.

Whereas many Israelis are interested in various philosophies and consider themselves to be open-minded, the Orthodox in general cut themselves off as much as possible from the modern world and don't mingle with people outside their own circle. Even those who wear embroidered *kippas*, but especially the black-coats, avoid speaking about Jesus and the New Testament, unless they are trying to draw back a Jew who has wandered from the fold.

So we were pleased when Barak and Abigail gladly accepted our tract.

By lunchtime we entered the Yatir Forest, the largest of Israel's planted forests. Although I had heard of it, I didn't grasp its dimensions until we began walking in it.

"It's so green!" John kept exclaiming.

"Yes, like the Carmel Mountains." I wondered why we'd never visited this beautiful place before.

"And do you realize we're still in the Negev Desert?"

Israel is the only country in the world that has reversed the process of deforestation. Geographically, Israel has long been a crossroads for armies sweeping through on campaigns throughout the Middle East. Most of the natural Mediterranean woods were obliterated by a long series of conquering powers, for the sake of agriculture and to provide fuel for early generations of steam locomotives on the Turkish-built railways. Today forests cover only three percent of Israel, one quarter the area they cover in Greece or Portugal. Yet far more trees grow here today than they did one hundred years ago, when Theodore Herzl, the founder of modern Zionism, proclaimed his vision for the formation of a Jewish homeland. Since the first trees were planted in Herzl's memory in 1908, over two hundred million have been added.

Forty years ago, when planting began in the Yatir Forest in the Judean foothills, experts argued it was impossible for trees to grow on the edge of the desert in such arid soil. The verdant woodland environment we were walking through proved how wrong they had been. We could hardly believe that just yesterday we were picking our way through jagged boulders with only a hint of green on the hills and an occasional poor flower struggling to survive in the stony ground.

The tangy aroma of pine trees and the lush smell of greenery enveloped us; the grass, studded with multi-colored flowers, formed a carpet next to the jeep road. As the trail proceeded up, down and around, we passed through stands of trees: pine, peach and pomegranate, carob and oak, almond, walnut and pistachio, along with grape vines. Each bend in the road yielded another visual treat.

We glimpsed anemone flowers for the first time. We were used to seeing anemones in the Galilee hills, but we weren't expecting to find them so far south. I know little about wildflowers, but the blood-red blossoms of the anemone are my favorite. They are one of the most impressive sights of the spring landscape. Seeing them dancing in the wind, I felt as if I'd met an old friend and we were smiling at each other.

Our Israel Trail book divides the trail into segments for short trips and the author rates them with one, two, or three stars, or none at all. One star is called "worthwhile," two stars are "suggested," and three are "required." The section through the Yatir Forest didn't rate even one star. The ratings are subjective; different people enjoy different types of scenery or hikes. But I wondered whether the author had trekked though here in the summer when everything was baked, barren and brown. And he surely wasn't from Eilat, which gives us a craving for anything green and blossoming.

We were surprised that we didn't meet anyone in the forest. Were people scared to tour here because of its proximity to the Palestinian Territories? Did they know something we didn't? We were used to seeing few people on the Trail, but in a stunning forest like this, it felt weird to be alone.

Only one road bisects the Yatir Forest. It serves as an access road to the small community of Shani on the northern border of the park, and continues to Arab towns and villages. We were heading toward that north/south artery where we expected to hitchhike out of the forest. But the trail seemed to go on interminably. Our map gave no indication that it would take so long, and after every turn we expected to see the paved road, our exit out of the forest.

I couldn't help noticing all the appealing groves and pleasant valleys we passed and thinking, *That would be a good place to camp*, or *We could probably put our tent up behind that thicket and no one would ever notice us*. But we had no choice; we had to reach the road and then we would hitchhike—something I was not looking forward to.

In my old, traveling hippy life, I had done some stupid things and camped in dangerous places. I had hitchhiked alone through Spain with its macho men, and stretched out in my sleeping bag a few meters off the road between olive trees in Yugoslavia. John liked to tell the story of how he had once slept on the sidewalk in front of a bank, under the overhang to get out of the rain. The young people hiking the Trail undeniably camped out even here, and if you didn't make a fire you would have less chance of being seen. But life was different now; we were older, wiser, and more responsible. I decided not to dwell on what I was missing by not camping, but try to enjoy our new style of hiking the *Shvil*.

Then we heard voices singing. We soon recognized a droning Arabic song. A Bedouin family came into view, piled on a cart behind a tractor, apparently on an outing to collect firewood. The man, dressed in western clothes, probably worked for the Jewish National Fund, the organization that manages the forests. Perhaps this was part of his job, because these forests demand much care: pruning, culling, gathering dead wood. The women wore long black embroidered dresses and white headscarves.

We waved at the family, the first people we had seen in hours. It was refreshing to see a family out together, obviously enjoying the surroundings.

We began to see picnic tables, garbage bins overflowing with plastic plates, empty soda bottles and newspapers. Here and there stood impressively-inscribed bronze plaques. "This grove was donated in memory of our dear father and mother ..."

Major contributors to the Jewish National Fund can have

their—or their loved ones—names recorded in commemorative inscriptions, a familiar feature of parks in Israel. We knew we must be drawing close to the road, because no one would want their plaque stuck out in the middle of an inaccessible forest, where it wouldn't be seen. It bothered me that people couldn't bestow money discreetly, without the fanfare of their name written in large letters. But then, realistically, the forests benefited and expanded.

We found the long-awaited road and it was anything but a major thoroughfare. The good thing about these kinds of roads for hitching is that if anyone does happen to come by, there's a good chance they'll pick you up. On the other hand, the road appeared to be deserted.

We began walking.

Soon a young Bedouin man in a Volkswagen van stopped and rolled down his window.

"Where're you going?" he asked, looking surprised to meet us in the middle of the forest. "Skiing?"

"We're on the Israel Trail, left Eilat nineteen days ago. We're on our way to Kibbutz Dan. Hope there's still snow on Mt. Hermon," John said. "Right now we're trying to get to friends in Omer."

His name was Hammed and he offered to drive us out of the forest to the main road to Beer Sheva from whence we shouldn't have trouble getting a ride. Just as I had suspected, with this new system of walking the *Shvil* our adventures didn't end when we stopped hiking for the day. Rather, a new adventure was just beginning—reaching our evening's destination.

Hammed dropped us at the junction and in five minutes an Arab man in a private car stopped. He had another gentleman in the front seat. The driver rolled down his window. "Where're you going?"

"Omer." We were still about ten kilometers away.

"Hop in the back and throw your packs in the trunk. That'll be ten *shekels* each."

We didn't mind paying, so we climbed into the car. Loud Arabic music blared on the radio.

"By the way, I have a few other stops to make," the driver informed us.

John and I looked at each other.

*This could be an interesting ride,* I thought.

We drove into the nearby Arab town of Hura and stopped to let off the other passenger. In the meantime, every time we passed someone standing along the road, even if he didn't motion for us to stop, our driver screeched to a halt, rolled down his window, and offered him a lift. We had discovered a new mode of transportation: the "unofficial taxi." The driver undoubtedly saved a lot of money by not paying for a taxi license and by not paying income tax, but I suspected that if he were discovered, he would be in major trouble with the law.

In a roundabout way, we finally reached Omer and found our friends' house. Their guest room turned out to be a luxurious suite, and we felt totally pampered, especially after a delicious home-cooked meal. John and I were certain we had shed a few kilos in our first eighteen days on the Trail. But I could see that our perfect weight loss diet—walking eight or ten hours a day and eating the most basic meals—would soon become a thing of the past.

Sitting in an easy chair with my feet up, I wrote in my diary the latest lessons I had learned:

- *I'm learning a new way of trusting God, not for a camping spot, but to get to the house where we'll sleep.*
- *We're blessed to be able to stay with friends—when else would we have such a chance?*
- *We can learn from receiving the hospitality of others rather than being the hosts as we usually are.*

Our problem of how to return to where we had left the Trail was solved when our host offered to drive us the next morning. I think we had overwhelmed him with our dazzling descriptions of the flowers, and he confessed that they hadn't been in the Yatir Forest for years, since the picnics they used to take there with their young children.

"Where do you think we'll stay tomorrow?" I asked.

John didn't answer.

"I just think we could call someone," I added. I appreciated when our guests informed us ahead of time that they were coming, and I tried to do the same for others.

"But we don't know how far we'll get exactly. Maybe we'll find a guest house on one of the *kibbutzim* we pass." The Trail made a wide circle north of the city of Beer Sheva.

I didn't want our sleeping arrangements to become a daily conflict between us, so I resolved to trust God's guidance as I had when we had searched for a camping spot in the desert.

We climbed into bed. I pulled the thick comforter up under my chin and relished the smell of clean sheets. John reached over and turned off the light. I wondered where we would be sleeping tomorrow.

# 9. Bushwhacking through Anemones

We discovered there were no *kibbutzim* with guest houses in the area, so we hitched back to Beer Sheva to stay with our friends, Tammy and Mike.

This trip required us to drive for nearly an hour south, in the direction we'd come from. I hoped that all our lodgings wouldn't take us so far from the Trail. We found Mike working in the Bible bookstore that he managed in the center of the city. Since he was busy when we arrived and told us he was expecting Tammy in an hour, we set off for the nearby shopping mall to get something to eat.

It had never occurred to me that I might stroll around a mall while on the Israel Trail. How did we get so far removed from nature? After twenty days on the *Shvil* I felt like a visitor from another planet, or like an anthropologist observing a new culture, as I gaped blankly at one shop after another.

My mind was still on the interesting encounter we'd had with a Bedouin family that morning behind the new Israeli town of Metar. The day had been warmer than we'd anticipated and our water supply was getting low. We saw three Bedouins gathering grass—a young man, a young woman dressed in a long skirt with a wool scarf over her head, and an older woman in a traditional black velvet dress with intricate embroidery and a thin white scarf draped down her back. The older woman had tattoos on her face. They were shearing the grass with sickles and stuffing it into burlap bags. Most Bedouin, even those who live in towns, keep animals next to their homes—goats, sheep, chickens, donkeys, camels, or horses.

The young man, who spoke Hebrew, introduced himself as Amin. We asked if they could spare us some water. They gave us a fresh bottle from their truck and insisted we accept oranges and bananas as well. Amin mentioned that he was having trouble finding work in the area.

"You can always find a job in Eilat," John told him. "Come to our hostel and you can stay for free. Here's a pamphlet with our information on it."

With typical Bedouin hospitality, they invited us to their home, but we told them we had to continue on our way.

The next morning, Friday, Tammy drove us to the Beer Sheva bus station, the transportation hub for southern Israel. As we sat on a bench waiting for a bus to take us north to where we'd stopped the previous day, we discovered that we were among only a handful of travelers in a throng of soldiers. Israel is such a small country that soldiers usually go home for the weekend several times a month. Two of our children had been stationed for part of their service in Beer Sheva, and I could imagine them here, running to catch a bus or sitting on one of the hard wooden benches with their friends. A number of years before, our son Josh happened to be in the Beer Sheva bus station a half-hour before a terrorist's bomb exploded. Terrorists frequently target bus stations, especially when they know many soldiers are present.

Being in the midst of hundreds, even thousands, of green and khaki uniforms was a unique experience. I thought about these young people setting aside two or three years of their lives to serve their country. I pictured many a mother looking forward to having her son or daughter home for the weekend and preparing their favorite *shabbat* meal. In Hebrew *shabbat* has the same root letters as the words "sit" and "rest." Orthodox religious families observe *shabbat* by not working, driving, or cooking from sundown on Friday to sundown on Saturday, but even non-religious families typically celebrate with a meal together on Friday evening.

Shortly after leaving the bus, as we walked through the fields around Kibbutz Dvira, breathing air filled with the pungent smell of cow sheds, a jogger trotted toward us.

"Shalom!" John greeted him.

The man's T-shirt was wet with perspiration. "Shalom!" he returned, bouncing in place.

*This guy is a serious jogger,* I thought. He acted as if he couldn't wait to get moving again.

"We're on the *Shvil*," John told him. "We started in Eilat and we're on our way to Dan. Today is our twenty-first day."

"No kidding! I've always wanted to walk the *Shvil*." He came to a standstill, temporarily forgetting his run. "My name's Itai. Maybe you'd like to come back to my house on the *kibbutz*?"

"Thanks, but we really have to keep going," John said. "It's still early. But here's something we wrote with our address in Eilat on it." We were continually surprised by the respect that we received for tackling the Israel Trail.

Farther along, we walked parallel to the railway tracks—not the most exciting part of the Trail, but the easy hike gave me time to think. At one point, as we walked between the train tracks and the highway, I reflected on the tremendous changes in transportation in the past two hundred years. From ancient times until the nineteenth century, if you wanted to get from one place to another, you simply stood up and started walking. If you were rich enough to have an animal you could go somewhat faster.

Bible stories were acquiring new dimensions for me. I thought about the Lord telling Abram in Genesis, "Leave your country,

your people and your father's household and go to the land I will
show you."

Sounds simple, but I could just envision Abraham, his family,
and their herds trekking all the way from Iraq to Beer Sheva. And
what about Moses followed by a couple million Israelites trooping
out of the land of Goshen on their way to the Promised Land, but
first wandering for forty years in the desert?

After Jesus was born in Bethlehem, an angel appeared to
Joseph and casually told him, "Get up, take the child and his
mother and escape to Egypt." On foot. The apostle Paul traipsed
all over the land that is now Israel, Lebanon, Syria, Turkey and
Greece; and in classic understatement wrote that he was "in danger
from rivers, bandits, in the city, and in the country."

For them, of course, it was normal to walk, and unless you
had a donkey, horse or camel, all you could take with you was
what you carried on your back—no suitcase, carry-on, or duffel
bag. An extra set of clothing was about the limit, plus a few
personal items. Life was simpler then.

On our hike we were discovering that time and distance take
on a totally different perspective when you are self-propelled. You
no longer think in terms of traveling one hundred kilometers an
hour or of making five hundred miles in a day. First you consider
the terrain that you have to cross. Are there many hills? If so, that
will surely slow you down. What about the weather? In a car, you
turn on your wipers and drive slower. But if it rains hard when you
are on foot, rivers may flood and you may have to stop completely.
Hot weather brings a different set of challenges.

Thankfully we were experiencing a beautiful warm day in the
Negev. Since we knew which direction to go, we took shortcuts
straight across fields instead of following the bows and bends of
Nahal Shikma, a long streambed that winds through the southeast
Mediterranean region. We passed along a *tel* that stuck up from the
grassland like a hump on a camel's back.

"Take a picture, Jupe," John said, posing in front of the huge green bulge, yellow flowers at his feet.

Innumerable undeveloped, potential archaeological sites exist in Israel. Some are obvious, such as this lonely *tel* in the middle of a plowed field. Thousands of others are still hidden. Archeologists are summoned every time a new building project begins. Every contractor fears that his construction crew will unearth an ancient cave, wall, or pot. If he's lucky, work will be suspended for a short time, though in other cases he may be forced to drastically change his plans.

Recently, for instance, an addition was being built onto the Megiddo prison in the north of Israel, and prisoners serving short-term sentences were helping with the excavations. Suddenly one of them was startled when the edge of his shovel uncovered a piece of an elaborate mosaic. Further digging revealed it to be the floor of a church. The symbol of the fish used by early Christians and an inscription to "the god, Jesus Christ" appeared. Some archaeologists are already hailing it as the world's oldest church, and more than sixty inmates are participating in the dig, having found a new outlet for their energy. A number have decided they want to pursue a career in archaeology when they are discharged. Jewish prisoners have testified that while uncovering this church, they felt they were on "holy ground." The Prisons Authority is less enthusiastic, left with the question of where to put the new prison wing.

Contractors consider it even worse luck to uncover ancient bones. The rabbis here take bones extremely seriously and all further construction is immediately stopped. First, archaeologists and historians must determine if they are Jewish bones, and if so, the bones must be given a proper Jewish burial. The process has been known to hold up the building of new roads for months.

Past the *tel*, we had to get from one side of the highway to the other. We could see where we had to go, but how would the

Trail take us there? Farther along we found markers indicating that the track led us through an underpass. Unfortunately it had rained recently, and the tunnel was flooded.

"What do you think, Jupe?" John asked. "Can we get through?" He took a few steps and sank into the mud. "Okay, no problem. We'll just cross the highway."

I tried not to say anything negative as we climbed up the bank. Cars were speeding down the four-lane freeway in both directions. But I thought, *How will we possibly get across?*

"When I say 'Go!'—make a run for it," directed John.

"Wait, wait!" Had we hiked for weeks on the Trail only to get run over by a semi-trailer? At that moment I would rather have been on a mountain ledge.

*Don't rush and push yourself into the traffic*, I told myself, just like when I was learning to drive. Eventually the gaps between the vehicles lengthened; I charged and made it across.

Safely on the other side, we crested a hill and were greeted by the sight of about thirty parked cars and the aroma of barbequed meat.

"Hey, it's *shabbat*," John reminded me. "Families are out taking trips." The Israeli weekend is only one day. It starts Friday afternoon and ends Saturday night.

"But why so many cars right here?" I wondered aloud.

A few more meters gave us our answer. We had walked into fields studded with thousands—millions—of anemones, red as blood.

We saw people walking along paths in every direction: couples walking arm-in-arm, parents pushing baby strollers, small children running ahead of their parents, boys throwing stones into the flood-water pond. Till now we hadn't met more than a couple of people a day, so we immediately felt self-conscious with our backpacks and walking poles. We discovered that encounters with hordes of people didn't necessarily lead to more conversations. When we met fellow hikers in the wilderness, we always greeted one another and eagerly exchanged information. But now it was as if we were slipping anonymously through a crowd.

We had to search carefully for the *Shvil* signs among the many paths, but we eventually found the old Turkish Bridge.

"Take a picture, Jupe."

We stacked our packs on top of each other and balanced the camera on them for a self-timed photo. This is the place we had first seen an Israel Trail sign on our trip home from Tel Aviv nine months ago. We could never have known then that we would be back so soon, on our twenty-first day of hiking the Israel Trail.

We took out the map.

"It's already afternoon and the Trail makes a huge circle before coming out to the road again," John said. "And it doesn't look like the most interesting route."

"So what d'you want to do?" I asked.

"Look, we can take a short cut and get to the same place a nicer way."

By following the Israel Trail we would have covered about seven kilometers, and by the direct route, we figured we would only walk about four, less than an hour's hike. Unfortunately we got lost within ten minutes after leaving the Turkish Bridge.

We crossed spectacular green pastures sprinkled with crimson anemones. Cattle and sheep, seemingly oblivious to their glorious surroundings, contentedly browsed on the red crown anemones. Compared to the herds in the Negev and Sinai who had only sparse dry bushes to feed on, these creatures were in animal heaven.

The fact that this land was used for grazing meant that we kept bumping into fences and couldn't follow the course we had planned on the map. John thrives on bushwhacking; he enjoys getting off the established route, whether hiking or living his life. But I was getting tired and wanted to find our familiar white, blue, and orange markers.

We were down in the Nahal Shikma streambed again. "Hey, over here," John called. "We have to get up higher where we can see something."

"I know, I know." I plunged into a dense thicket of thorny brambles up to my armpits.

"Just follow in my steps, and I'll forge a way through here," John said. But as soon as he took a step forward, the thistles sprang back into their place, covering all traces of John and forcing me to create my own path.

*How did we get ourselves into this mess?*

This wasn't what I envisioned when I planned our Israel Trail hike. My energy level was flagging. A granola bar would help. If only we had stayed on the marked trail! We might have made a wide turn around but at least I would be spared these scratches and would know where I was.

Finally we came to a grove of trees on a hill and could locate our position. A half-hour later we were out on the highway.

Later I thought, *People who spend their lives wandering around with no direction often feel they are walking through brambles and into walls, and they don't see the way out.*

Being lost for a few hours and away from the Israel Trail markers made me realize how thankful I was that God gave me direction in my life when I chose to follow Him thirty years ago.

Once out on the road we managed to get to Rehovot by bus and taxi, and we had a restful and encouraging weekend with our friends Jack and Judi.

I wrote in my diary:

- *Our bodies can really use a day of rest.*
- *Don't become complacent even when the trail is flat and boring.*
- *The trail, as in life, often takes unexpected turns, and if we're not paying attention, we can easily go astray.*

A bus ride on Sunday morning took us back to where we left
off, to Moshav Ahuzam. We stepped off at the entrance to the
community and walked through the *moshav* (cooperative village)
expecting to find the trail signs on the other side.

As the dirt road led us out into the brush, we discovered that
a large area of the land was completely torn up. A new road was
being built. The construction workers certainly wouldn't notice the
*Shvil* signs, and how often did the Trails committee come through
to verify that the markers were in the right places? The few signs
we found pointed in opposite directions.

We walked on one road for a couple of kilometers until we
felt we were heading in the wrong direction, and then went back
to where we started.

"This is nonsense," said John, who hates to backtrack. "Let's
just go back to that first road."

I still wasn't sure it was the correct route, and because of the
clouds we couldn't tell which direction we were going. Maybe we
should have taken a compass for times like this.

"Come on, there's no other choice," John said. "This must
be the right way."

We walked on in silence, me trying not to fret and John totally
confident. Soon we came to an orange grove and saw three men in
a pickup truck inspecting the fruit-laden trees.

"Shalom!" John greeted them. "We're on the Israel Trail,
our twenty-second day since leaving Eilat. Do you know where it
passes around here?"

One man pointed us in a direction that I felt was wrong.

"Thanks!" said John, striding on down the dirt road in the
indicated direction. I followed him, grumbling.

"These men probably don't even know the *Shvil* exists."

We walked about three kilometers, in "faith," when to my
relief we saw a familiar three-colored marker on a eucalyptus tree.

"Time for a snack," I announced. Now I could enjoy my

granola bar and orange.

The trail led us through rolling wheat fields, the dark green blades waving gently in the wind. We weren't in a purely natural landscape like the desert, but I still found it appealing. As we approached the vineyards surrounding Moshav Lachish, a light drizzle began to fall. We were enjoying perfect hiking weather, if the rain didn't become stronger. The area around Lachish is renowned for its grapes, and we were sorry to be hiking through when the twisted vines were brown and dry, rather than heavy with luscious fruit.

Tel Lachish rose tall and impressive above the surrounding countryside. Although far from any large town today, Lachish had been an important city in the past, as evidenced by the height and size of the *tel*. When Joshua led the Israelites into the Promised Land, Lachish was already established and had its own king. Archaeologists have confirmed that a destruction took place in 1200 B.C., a period when Lachish wasn't surrounded by a wall. This is the same time that the Bible says the primitive, rag-tag Israelite warriors conquered it.

As we circumvented the expansive *tel*, John reminded me that Lachish was where Sennacharib confronted the nation of Judah during the reign of King Hezekiah. That this mighty king of Assyria chose to lay siege to Lachish after making war on Jerusalem in 701 B.C., shows how strategically important this city was. The Assyrian siege ramp is still visible today, leading up from the parking lot.

We were walking along a pleasant dirt road and could tell we weren't far from the main road, our destination, when suddenly we both had the same thought.

*Where are the markers?*

As usual, I got the map out to see where we went wrong. We had been enjoying the easy track so much that we failed to notice that the Israel Trail took a sharp right turn.

"Shall we go back to look?" I suggested.

John didn't hesitate. "Nah, if we head through this wheat field we'll pick up the *Shvil* on the other side. It's no big deal. Follow me!"

Walking through thigh-high wheat becomes tiring after a while. I hoped the farmer wouldn't mind that we trampled down some of his wheat stalks.

Soon a restaurant next to a gas station came into view, looking terribly attractive. Before leaving Eilat, I had imagined that we would find little snack bars or ice cream trucks periodically along the Trail. But in fact, this was one of the first times we could have a cup of tea after our day's hike. And we needed to stop and consider where to stay the night. I hated having to deal with this question every day.

"Racheli said she wanted to walk with us sometime," I said. "If she doesn't have to study tomorrow, we could sleep at her place and then take off tomorrow morning together."

"Okay, send her a message on my cell phone."

Racheli's reply that she would be happy for us to stay with her aroused my motherly emotions. We decided that it would be worth traveling some extra kilometers to stay with our daughter.

"I wonder how the buses run from here," I mused, "it doesn't seem like a busy road."

"Well, I've hardly got any shekels left anyway," announced John, "so we'll just hitch." John took care of our money.

*How could he get us into this situation?* I wondered. *No money?!* I wasn't in the mood to hitchhike and could feel myself developing a rotten attitude.

Having no choice, we began walking and hitching and eventually arrived at Racheli's after over an hour on the road, with rides from two cars and a shared taxi. John was energized by all the people he could talk to. I was looking forward to hiking with Racheli and her friend Karen tomorrow.

\* \* \*

The next morning as we began our day together, it was fun for us to point out the tri-colored Israel Trail signs to Racheli and Karen and to enlist their help in finding them.

Technically, the markers should be in sight of each other. On a wide, straight path they would be farther apart, whereas on a winding trail or one with many trees or rocks, they'd be closer. In practice though, we often had to search for them and four eyes were better than two.

We enjoyed  introducing the girls to what had become our routine for the past twenty-three days. As students used to being confined indoors, they were thrilled to get outside and into nature. I felt like a hostess anxious to make a good impression on her guests; I was delighted to discover that our hike today led through stunningly beautiful country scenery. Ample winter rains had covered this region, the foothills of the Judean Hills, in a blanket of dazzling green sprinkled thickly with our favorite anemones.

"Wow, we should do this more often." Racheli said.

My heart was soaring like the ravens in the sky above us. All parents love to see their children absorbing and emulating their interests, passions, and way of life.

"I can't believe what I'm missing by not getting out of the city," Karen exclaimed.

Everywhere I looked there was beauty; the anemones beckoned me to photograph them.

Racheli and Karen kept us moving at a quick pace. John and I were used to pacing ourselves in order to keep going for eight, nine, or ten hours.

After about an hour Racheli offered to trade packs with me.

*What a daughter!* I thought. My pack wasn't terribly heavy any more, but I felt liberated as I placed her much lighter day pack on my shoulders.

Walking through the foothills we came to the top of ridges where we had spectacular views over to the coast; we could even see Tel Aviv in the distance.

"Can you believe that we'll get to Tel Aviv in about five days?" John said.

"Yeah, did you ever hear of anyone walking to Tel Aviv? Even by road it's 350 kilometers."

"And a few days later we'll be at the Ong's house in Caesarea," added John. "You'll like that." Daniel and Eunice Ong are friends of ours from Singapore who live in one of the wealthiest communities in Israel.

Though we had left our camping gear in Arad, we had decided to keep our cooking pot, tea and coffee with us; but in fact, we had hardly used them anymore. Today, however, we wanted the girls to have an authentic Trail experience. Racheli and Karen thoroughly enjoyed our campfire on a high, grassy slope and the coffee to go with our sandwiches. We had been hiking through a countryside of scraggly, prickly bushes and low trees, but here we rested in a delightful clearing.

Our route took us over Tel Azeka, another of Israel's national parks. It was strange to be walking through such an organized area with many marked trails, picnic tables and even sturdy wooden benches to sit on and admire the view. The Israel Trail truly does cross a great variety of landscapes.

From one of the overlooks we could gaze straight down into the Valley of Ela. I imagined the Philistine and the Israelite armies confronting each other when Goliath strode onto the battlefield. At the time of King Saul, the Philistines controlled the southern coastal region of Israel, which was part of the territory that the Israelites failed to conquer during the time of the Judges. Israel paid dearly for her disobedience, and the Philistines became a continual source of trouble for God's people. The land of Judah higher up in the hills made the Valley of Ela a natural battleground between the two nations. Some scholars believe that during the renowned conflict of David and Goliath, the Philistine camp stood on this hill of Azeka. The Israelite camp was believed to be stationed on the opposite hill, called Lupine Hill today, due to the prevalence in the springtime of the striking purple flowers.

Without lingering long on top, we set off down the hill to examine the meandering *wadi* from which David must have taken the "five smooth stones" that he used to smite the mighty Goliath.

The girls had yet to experience one aspect of walking the *Shvil*—getting lost. From the beginning of our day together I could tell that Racheli's approach to hiking was more like John's than like mine. After not seeing a marker for what I considered a reasonable distance, I inevitably began looking around uneasily asking, "Anyone seen a trail sign?"

Racheli would give me one of her "Give me a break, Mom" looks and say something like, "Come on, take it easy."

But as we headed down into the Valley of Ela, Karen set off in the lead, bounding down a trail without paying attention to whether it was the right one or not. We all followed. Soon enough even Racheli and Karen had to acknowledge that we had lost our way. From the top of the hill, we had had a clear view of where we were supposed to end up, but the problem of how to get there had all of us searching for the trail signs. Now they had experienced this aspect of hiking the Israel Trail. After we all went sliding down a bluff, John stepped into the lead and managed to put us back on track.

An occasional oak or carob tree spread its branches above the Roman ruins. The trail wound its way between ancient arches, lintels, pillars, cisterns, and wine presses. For such a well-kept area in the peak of the wildflower season, we were surprised not to have met any other people until this part; but then we met a group of school children on top of Hurvat Tzura: three male teachers with about twenty eighth-grade boys.

"Hey," one of the taller boys greeted us, "where are you going? Skiing?!" He stared at our walking sticks. The rest of the class chuckled at what seemed to them a hilarious, original joke.

"Yeah, we're on our way to Mt. Hermon, "John replied, warming to his audience."We're on the Israel Trail—started in Eilat; now on our twenty-third day."

The boys and teachers gathered in a circle around us.

"All of you?"

"Only my parents," responded Racheli who, carrying my backpack, looked like a genuine hiker. "The two of us joined them for the day."

"You're not joking, are you?" one boy asked.

I decided that I had a tremendous respect for any person who took it upon himself to be a teacher, particularly to eighth-grade boys. We learned that they were from a school in the nearby small town of Kiryat Malachi, and that one of the teachers, Uzi, knew my cousin who was from a neighboring *moshav*.

"Here's a pamphlet we wrote about our walk." John offered the teachers our tract. "We're Messianic Jews."

"Wow, I respect you for that," said Uzi.

Racheli and Karen looked at each other as if they couldn't believe this conversation was taking place.

"Please, please, take a picture with us!" the boys demanded, arranging themselves around us. Our girls were beaming, enjoying their new super-hiker status.

Messianic Jews are more accepted today in Israel than a generation ago, but we are still prepared for negative reactions when we tell people we believe that Jesus—*Yeshua*—is the Messiah. Many Israelis affirm that a Jew can believe in whatever he wants—Buddha, Hinduism, New Age, or atheism—and still be Jewish, as long as he doesn't believe in Jesus. Some ultra-Orthodox groups even react violently to meetings of Messianic Jews, through demonstrations, putting up posters, or throwing stones. This, however, is not the norm.

While acknowledging that Jesus was Jewish, most Israelis would connect belief in Him as a betrayal of one's roots or as the acceptance of something foreign. Tragically, part of the responsibility for this extreme attitude rests with Christianity. Before I became a follower of Jesus, I believed, as most Jews do, that the Crusaders, Hitler, and the Nazis were all Christians. I didn't know the difference between institutionalized Christianity or Christians in name only, and true followers of Jesus.

"Look what they've done in the name of Jesus," Israelis will say. "So how can I believe in Him?"

Paul, an Orthodox Jew before he received a revelation of Jesus Christ and became an apostle, wrote in the Epistle to the Romans, "Salvation has come to the Gentiles to make Israel envious," (Rom. 11:11). In many instances the opposite has occurred, as Jews have been persecuted in Jesus' name. The rabbis, who are outstanding scholars, have spent two thousand years perfecting arguments against Jesus.

After seven hours on the trail Racheli and Karen were exhausted. Seeing them dragging their feet and slowing their pace, John and I smiled at each other as we realized the fitness level we had acquired in twenty-three days.

"We'll take a short-cut out to the highway through that grove of almond trees," John decided.

The next day we would be trekking up the long, twisty ascent to Jerusalem. I wasn't sure where we would sleep, though we had many friends there; and I didn't relish the idea of entering Israel's capital. Reaching Jerusalem was a milestone for our journey, but I wanted to avoid cities when possible.

The trail skirts Jerusalem's western edge. I didn't think I could bear riding on city buses and being caught up in traffic jams; but where else could we stay? Would a 25-K hike to Moshav Yad Hashmona, where we also had friends, be too much for one day? Could we bypass Jerusalem altogether? Probably not.

I wrote in my diary:

- *The girls were great to have with us for company. So much fun to have along, and they totally enjoyed the day. Got quickly into looking for the signs.*
- *Tomorrow looks to be a very long, hard day. Lord, help us.*

# 10. Up to Jerusalem & Down Again

Jerusalem radiates a particular mystique. Most first-time visitors find their sojourn there an extraordinary experience; Lonely Planet, the popular series of travel guides for backpackers, calls Jerusalem, "perhaps the most fascinating city in the world and one of the most beautiful." The population of Jerusalem is unique because it includes many ultra-Orthodox Jews and one third of the residents are Muslim. The climate is cool with a low humidity for most of the year; the white limestone architecture is beautiful.

In biblical times Jewish men were commanded to appear in the Temple in Jerusalem three times a year for the Feasts. Jesus, when he was twelve years old, "went up to Jerusalem according to the custom of the feast." The Hebrew expression *aliya* ("going up") has both a spiritual and physical meaning. In Psalm 122 it is written that Jerusalem is a city where "the tribes *go up* to the Testimony of Israel." After the Babylonian captivity "everyone whose heart God had moved prepared to *go up* and build the house of God in Jerusalem" (Ezra 1:5). Jerusalem is mentioned by name 807 times in the Bible and referred to another seventy times.

To arrive in Jerusalem from either the east or the west, one literally has to go up through the region of Israel called the Judean Hills. Jerusalem stands about eight hundred meters above sea level and on all sides is surrounded by *wadis* and valleys. When you travel by car you pass through striking scenery on the way up to Jerusalem, but you don't appreciate the full meaning of the word *aliya* until you ascend on foot.

Jerusalem for me is special in a personal way. Besides the fact that I received my first Bible in Jerusalem, I also met John there. The day after accepting the Bible, Christmas 1973, I was hitchhiking with a friend back to our hut on the Sinai coast, when a van picked us up outside of Bethlehem. A short distance farther on, the car stopped for two more hitchhikers, a girl and a guy with long blond hair, cut-off jean shorts, worn-out sandals held together with pieces of wire, and a big smile on his face. We began talking and soon he was telling us about his faith in Jesus.

"Wow! I just got a Bible today. I plan to read it in Nueiba," I said. "I'm living there under some palm trees on the beach."

"Cool," he answered. "My name's John. I'll come down to visit you. I live in a hut outside Eilat."

The van driver dropped the four of us off in Beer Sheva. I didn't see John again until six months later when I was living with an elderly couple in Jerusalem who invited young people to stay and study the Bible with them. One day the doorbell rang and when I opened it, the blond man I'd met hitchhiking stood before me.

John barely recognized me—my whole appearance and countenance had changed. The first time he saw me I was wearing a long black Bedouin dress, with multiple rings, bracelets, and charms on my hands, wrists, and neck. This time the jewelry was gone, and I had on a simple skirt and shirt. In any case, he wasn't expecting to see me at a Bible study.

John and I began spending time together, and nine months after that second meeting, we married in the U.S.

Those memories flooded back as John and I made our ascent to Jerusalem, one of the harder Trail segments. I set my mind for a serious uphill climb this day. Before we left home I was concerned about the weather on this stretch of the Trail, because Jerusalem is often cold and rainy in the winter. Snow even falls in Jerusalem about once a year. In vain I had searched for a poncho in the Beer Sheva mall, thinking we would need it on our climb up to Jerusalem. The morning of our ascent I was delighted to awaken to a perfect day—neither cold nor hot—with sparse friendly clouds floating in the sky. *Why do I waste my time worrying?* I thought. *In the end, things always worked out.*

On our map the trail through the Judean Hills looked curvy and complicated, but we found that since we were walking most of the day through Jewish National Forests, we were usually on straightforward, well-marked paths. With wooden signposts appearing regularly, we scarcely needed to consult our map.

Early in the day we passed the two-thousand-year-old Roman Steps; they are still clearly distinguishable. I wondered out loud, "Where did they lead? And why were they exactly at this point?"

The incline was steep, but were steps really necessary? From what ruins remained, John and I could only speculate. Perhaps Jesus used these same paths with His disciples. During His three years of public ministry He went frequently up to Jerusalem for the feasts.

I stooped to pick some *zaatar*, or wild thyme, which grew in abundance all over the hills. It felt oily when rubbed between my fingers, and it smelled like a pot of spaghetti.

According to our map, the Israel Trail section around the village of Matah, a village in the Judean Hills about ten kilometers from Jerusalem, was uncomplicated; however, we soon found ourselves in a construction zone. Matah was evidently expanding and its new perimeter fence cut right through the *Shvil*. With no trail signs visible, we followed our instincts and tried to carry on in the same direction. As we hugged the edge of the settlement, we noticed a thin wire strung between the utility poles encircling

Matah. It was an *eruv*, which is meant to define the area in which a religious Jew is allowed to carry belongings on the Sabbath.

The rabbis believe that the prohibition in the *Torah* (the first five books of the Bible) against working on the *shabbat* includes carrying things from one "domain," as they call it, to the other. Only within one's own home is this law suspended. The rabbis are extremely clever and look for ways around the commands. They believe they must follow the letter of the law precisely, but they are not adverse to using modern technology or other manipulations to make their lives easier. In the case of the *eruv*, the wire is meant to allow observant Jews to treat an entire neighborhood or settlement as if it were their mutual "home," and thus to be free from the hardships imposed by the law.

After this, we looked for the *eruv* when we went around towns and villages, *kibbutzim* and *moshavim*, so we could recognize religious settlements. This became part of a game we played as we hiked along. And in Arab towns we scanned the skyline for either a church steeple or a mosque to know if it was home to Christians, Muslims, or both.

We loved hiking through the tumbled-down ruins and the stone terraces built into the hills that indicated this area had been heavily settled in the past. The terraces were the perfect system for farming on steep, rocky terrain. Ancient farmers had cleared the stones from the soil and used them to build walls to hold more soil, thus forming small, flat plots. Olive, almond, and carob trees pushed up from between the stones. Prickly pear hedges served as time-worn fences around former villages.

Who moved all the rocks to build these extraordinary terraces? How many centuries old were they? Could they have been built when the tribe of Judah settled here during the conquest under Joshua? Other buildings, with their arched doorways, appeared to be Crusader architecture; some remains seemed to be from abandoned Arab villages.

After lunch we entered the Begin Park, named after Israel's former Prime Minister, Menachem Begin. The trail zigged and zagged among ridges and valleys. We weren't familiar with this area, but by car we were probably only fifteen minutes from Jerusalem. As in the Yatir Forest days ago, the trail was more winding and much longer than it looked on the map. We began a long descent into a dense, dark forest gorge.

While striding along a jeep trail, we saw a religious man about our age approaching us, the first person we had seen all day. He was wearing a black suit, large black *kippa*, long white beard and side curls; he looked like a fish out of water. John and I looked at each other wondering how this religious Jew would respond if we mentioned Yeshua.

As he approached, he greeted us, stopped, and began asking questions. "Where are you going? What's the Israel Trail? Why the poles?" At least he didn't ask if we were going skiing.

John explained to him about the *Shvil*, and told him he had knee problems and the poles took the pressure off his knees. Our new friend, who was unusually talkative and friendly, told us that he also had knee problems since his army service with the paratroopers. From this we deduced that he hadn't always been so orthodox, otherwise he would have been exempt from the army. He wanted to know where he could buy poles like ours, and John referred him to a camping store.

"Do you mind if I join you?" he asked.

Of course we didn't. So he turned around 180 degrees with us and soon was marching alongside us with John's sticks. Knowing that Jewish religious men are not in the habit of speaking to women, I walked in silence listening to the conversation.

He told us his name was Ephraim and that he sometimes felt the need to escape from the confinement of the *yeshiva* and to experience the presence of God in nature. John shared that our journey was, among other things, a spiritual pilgrimage as we sought to draw closer to God, our Creator and our Savior. The men traded quotations from the Scriptures, John citing verses from the Old Testament and Ephraim using examples from the Talmud, a record of rabbinic discussions on Jewish law, ethics, customs, legends, and stories, which Jewish tradition places on an equal footing with the Old Testament. The conversation flowed easily and I sensed that our friend enjoyed speaking to someone who, though not appearing outwardly to be devout, was clearly interested in the things of God.

Then John asked Ephraim how he viewed the Messiah. When he gave him a roundabout, ambiguous answer, John quoted one of his favorite Bible verses from Isaiah 53: "We all, like sheep, have gone astray, each of us has turned to his own way; and the Lord has laid on him the iniquity of us all."

"Do you think this could refer to the Messiah?" John asked.

Again Ephraim responded with the type of obscure explanation for which rabbis are famous. "It's not so simple," he said. "There are many possible explanations for this passage. For instance, some of our sages believe this chapter is speaking about the nation of Israel. Others believe it could be one of the prophets—Isaiah or Jeremiah, for instance. And which Messiah? We see two Messiahs in the Bible."

At least he wasn't specialized in rebuttals against the verses of Scripture that we believe refer to Jesus, or he could have become defensive. I was proud of the gentle way John was handling their dialogue.

We arrived at Ein Kobi, a lovely spring surrounded by pines, fig trees, and sycamores. While the men sat on a stone bench and continued their discussion, I explored the surroundings—a spring bubbling up into an underground reservoir and pools built from hewn stones—and decided this place was a hidden gem.

I returned to see Ephraim holding one of our tracts and speaking on his cell phone with his wife.

"Can you come over here to Ein Kobi? There's a couple here who are like us and I'd like you to meet them."

Perhaps his wife was used to his unusual escapades. In any case she declined, saying that she wasn't feeling well. In parting, John invited Ephraim to the Shelter with an offer to stay for free.

Shortly after leaving Ein Kobi we passed close to the Hadassah Hospital on the outskirts of Jerusalem. We paused to take a picture through the pine trees of the shining white apartment blocks and the cranes rising above building sites. Another milestone on our journey—we had walked to Jerusalem.

We were traveling along the section of the *Shvil* called the Springs Trail, a hike of several kilometers. We passed one water source after another, each one a complex of tunnels, pools, and aqueducts. At dusk we arrived at a sign that read, Sataf; it pointed up a seemingly endless series of uneven stone steps. The pale almond blossoms growing on terraced slopes lifted my spirits as I stumbled up exhausted to the well-preserved pools and stone buildings of Sataf. From far down the hill we could hear the shouts of children. Sataf, an ancient village which contains the remains of the oldest agriculture in the region, is easily approachable from the road above, making it a favorite destination for school trips. Archaeologists have found remnants from 4000 B.C. showing that grapes, pomegranates, olives, and figs were raised here. At the site we found teenagers splashing in the watery tunnels; no one noticed two tired hikers passing through with backpacks and poles.

Exhausted and in no mood to hitchhike, I was grateful to step on a bus going to Moshav Yad Hashmona, a community of believers. It was dark when we arrived, so we went straight to the dining room to greet our friends, Yonatan and Damaris, who had walked a portion of the Trail the previous year, then we crashed on our bed in their guest house. It had been a long day. We'd traveled about twenty-six kilometers, mostly uphill.

"Can you believe it, Jupe?" John said before he dozed off.

"We walked to Jerusalem in twenty-four days. Who ever walks to Jerusalem?"

In the morning another friend, Tzuri, drove us back to the Trail. The previous day we had walked up to Jerusalem. Today we would be going down to the foothills again. Much of the day we hiked on easy jeep trails, passing through green *wadis* filled with flowering almond trees. The almond tree is a harbinger of spring—it's one of the first trees to bloom after winter, seeming to convey a message of hope: the deadness of winter is over and life is returning to the land.

Soon the sound of heavy machinery came drifting through the trees. Who was disturbing our peace and quiet? Were motorcycles or quad runners allowed in this forest? As we advanced on the trail the racket increased, until we came upon a couple of men slicing logs with a chain saw, another on a tractor, and two others sitting next to a campfire preparing coffee in a blackened pot. They were Arabs from Hebron who were working for the Jewish National Fund. Israel's forests, because most of them are not natural but planted, require pruning and maintenance to keep healthy. Achmed, the spokesman, was friendly and he could read Hebrew, so we gave him a tract and invited him to Eilat.

We were passing through an area overlooking the Burma Road, also known as "The Road of Heroism," named after the road built by the Allies in World War II, to move troops from Burma to Japanese-controlled China.

This road that later memorialized that event, had been important in Israel's War of Independence in 1948. The *Shvil* here joined a guided trail, with placards describing the events that transpired here and monuments to the fallen soldiers.

At the time that the State of Israel was declared in 1948, approximately one hundred thousand people were living in West

Jerusalem. Arab armies besieged the city and few convoys were able to get through to its inhabitants with food and ammunition. Food was severely rationed and people faced starvation. Furthermore, without ammunition, the inhabitants of Jerusalem were vulnerable to enemy attacks. A plan was drawn up to quickly construct a make-shift road that would bypass the main road through the rugged, trackless mountains.

It had taken the Turks eight years to construct a road from Jerusalem to Jaffa in the nineteenth century, and under the British Mandate, which began in 1917, a similar road had taken two years to build. But with the critical situation in Jerusalem the young nation didn't have the time to build a proper highway. Working under cover of night in the range of Arab mortar, poorly equipped soldiers, elderly volunteers, students, super-Orthodox, and friendly local Arabs labored to maneuver boulders in the steep Judean Hills. On June 9, 1948, eight weeks after the road construction began, the lifeline to Jerusalem was completed just days before the United Nations negotiated a cease-fire. The Burma Road remains a symbol of courage to this day.

At one of the key military lookouts, called *Mishlat* 21, a green bench under an olive tree invited us to sit and admire the view.

"That's Modi'in," I said to John. "Can you believe we'll reach there in a couple of days?" I paused to absorb again the scope of our undertaking. The 325-kilometer drive from Jerusalem to Eilat takes about four hours.

"Yeah," he said. "Apart from seriously bad weather or problems at home, we've got a pretty good chance of finishing our journey."

Arriving at the road at 3:30 P.M. we called my cousin, Gershon, who lived close by and graciously came to pick us up. Thankfully I don't have a problem sleeping in a different bed every night and, after getting over the disappointment of not camping any more, I was enjoying the experience of staying with different friends.

In my diary I listed qualities—besides health, fitness, and motivation—that one needs to walk the Trail:

- *The ability to read maps*
- *Some sense of direction*
- *Camping skills*

The next day we invited Gershon to hike with us. He loves nature but doesn't get out as often as he would like, so he was delighted to have an excuse. Gershon decided from the outset that when he became tired, he would call his wife, Ofie, to come pick him up and to bring us our packs. We were still carrying our backpacks, because even without the sleeping bags, tent, and ground pads, we had our change of clothes, shoes, water bottle, lunch for the day, and other items. So it was a relief when we could be free of them.

From his first minute on the Trail, Gershon adored everything about it: the scenery, the exercise, being outdoors, looking for the markers, and leaving the cares of daily life behind for a few hours. He tried out John's poles, found them useful, and decided he would buy a pair. Gershon appreciated the steady pace we set; he felt himself getting in better shape with each step. He was already planning to join us again farther along on the *Shvil*.

Walking with Gershon was like taking a lesson in botany; he knows the name of every flower and plant, and is keen to point them out. Whereas normally we stride rapidly down paths through the woods, now we were noticing different varieties of orchids, anemones, cyclamens and ferns. We learned that the fields of waist-high yellow flowers were wild mustard.

"Try this," invited Gershon, popping one in his mouth.

For some reason I was surprised that when I chewed the flowers, I tasted the pungent spiciness of mustard; only the hotdogs were missing.

Wooden signposts indicated that we were passing through more important sites of the Independence War. Placards explained the significance of the places we passed. Not having grown up in Israel, I had missed the historical background that every child learns in school, and I was enjoying learning about Israel's history.

After 2½ hours of walking we reached the region of Latrun, halfway along the road between Tel Aviv and Jerusalem. Located in the Ayalon Valley, it's believed to be the place where Joshua commanded the sun to stand still during the battle between Israel and the five kings of the Amorites. Later, a succession of Maccabees, Romans, Crusaders, Arabs, and British all marched through this locale on their way up to Jerusalem. Some of the fiercest fighting of Israel's War of Independence took place in Latrun.

According to tradition, Latrun is the place where Jesus appeared to two of His disciples after His resurrection; the remains of the Emmaus Church are here. Emmaus is the name of the village, eleven kilometers from Jerusalem, where the two disciples were heading when they met the resurrected Jesus.

Latrun is also known for the imposing Trappist Monastery, known as the "Silent Monastery." Jokes abound in Israel about how the monks aren't allowed to speak, but in fact their vow of silence was annulled in 1960. The monks' vow of abstinence from alcohol apparently doesn't interfere with their famous winery; the monks use grapes grown in the surrounding vineyards to make the wine they sell in their small shop.

On a hill behind the monastery lie the ruins of a Crusader fortress. A community of German Christians has converted some of the remains into a simple, attractive guest house. The *Shvil* practically passes through its front yard. We stopped to say hello to our friend Nissim who had given Arnon, whom we met on our first day of the Trail, the address of the Shelter. My cousin Gershon was impressed with the buildings, the gardens, and the serene atmosphere. When Stephan, one of the members of the community, invited us for lunch, we couldn't refuse, and Gershon called Ofie to invite her to come see his new discovery, so close to their home.

"You're here already?" Ofie asked, when she arrived. "With Gershon and his plants, I thought it might take you all day."

I enjoyed the lunch, which included home-grown olives and lemonade made from their own trees, but I couldn't help glancing periodically at my watch and calculating how long we would need to walk to the town of Modi'in, our end point. Stephan was fascinated with Gershon's knowledge of flowers and his descriptions of expansive meadows of anemones in the south. He invited us for coffee after the meal, hoping for a more detailed explanation of how to find the impressive flower fields.

John was leaning back in his chair, totally relaxed. After a two-hour lunch break, however, I couldn't sit still any longer.

"Sorry, we'll have to skip the coffee," I blurted out.

I wondered if I was being too uptight, but John hadn't studied the map and wasn't aware of the distance we still had to cover. Ofie also wanted to move on, so Gershon invited Stefan to his house to hear more about anemones.

Gershon assured us that they would hike another trail section with us farther north. Nissim told us he would keep an eye out for more *Shvil* walkers, and we left a few of our pamphlets with him. We said good-bye to everyone, lifted our packs on our backs and finally set off again.

The Ben Shemen Forest seemed to go on and on, and the sun was nearly setting. I was glad we hadn't stayed for coffee. Catching our breath for a moment, we sat down on rocks under a twisted olive tree and I took a picture of the flaming sunset. We were beginning to hear the far-off hum of traffic. When would we reach the road? My legs were dragging; I didn't like being on the Trail so late, and we still needed to somehow get to our friends' house in Modi'in.

John sensed my mood and saw me eyeing my watch. "We're here!" John announced cheerily, looking at his watch. "5:17! Don't you hear the cars?"

Of course I heard them. I'd been hearing them for a while already, but to me they still sounded far away, and no road was in sight. I tried to suppress a negative attitude. I wished that John would understand that his premature optimism in declaring our arrival only upset me further.

In the semi-darkness a group of soldiers ran by us, huffing. Was this a sign that we were nearly there?

"Hi guys!" John said. "We're on the *Shvil Israel*, day twenty-six from Eilat." They hardly paused, though John did succeed in giving a few of our tracts to their officers who drove by a few minutes later in a jeep.

After what felt like an hour, but was really about fifteen minutes, I could finally start to make out the movement of cars between the trees. It was 5:30 P.M., nine hours after we had started. On the bus to Modi'in John spoke to the driver and a few passengers about our walk and gave them tracts.

We were at a turning point in our journey. We had passed the desert, the Judean Hills and Jerusalem, and the foothills. From now on until after Haifa we would be traveling through more populated country. I wondered how the Trail would guide us through the center of Israel. How could a hiking trail pass through a metropolis of a million people? It would definitely be a different kind of experience.

# 11. Trekking through the Metropolis

Israel is a tiny country the size of New Jersey and half the size of Holland, and its most populous region is pinched to a narrow sliver of land only fifteen kilometers wide. To relieve the bottleneck, the Israeli government designed an ambitious road construction plan to divert traffic around Tel Aviv and connect the periphery with the center of the country.

When the creators of the Israel Trail envisioned a hiking path through Israel, I doubt they had reckoned on the building of the Trans-Israel Highway, Route 6. I remember hearing, in the late 1990s, about the controversy surrounding the highway. The green parties were against appropriating farm and wilderness land for a highway, while the Transportation Ministry felt it was necessary for Israel's development.

I paid little attention to the debate. Now as we set out for a day walking parallel to Israel's first toll road, I could imagine the planners of the *Shvil* hearing about the highway and viewing its layout on the map.

"Oh, no," they must have lamented. "How do we get around this mess?!"

But once the highway became a reality, they had no choice but to get on with their job and design a way to bring hikers through the metropolis. On the map, our route this day didn't look like it had the most spectacular scenery, but since it was part of Israel, I was curious to discover what it had to offer.

Zela, our hostess, drove us from their home in Modi'in to the trailhead. Modi'in is a fast-growing planned city only ten years old, located between Jerusalem and Tel Aviv. With its abundant parks, wide boulevards, and terraced buildings, the city has a bright, modern atmosphere.

Ancient Modi'in was the home of the Maccabees, a priestly family whose name is associated with Hanukkah, the Feast of Lights. Judah Maccabee and his four brothers led a Jewish guerilla force in the battle against the ruling Greeks in the second century B.C. The tyrannical king, Antiochus, had initiated a program of Hellenization that sought to force the Jews to abandon their monotheism and to accept the Greeks' paganism. "Maccabee" is derived from the Hebrew word for "hammer"; they were said to strike hammer blows against their enemies. The revolt against cultural and religious assimilation eventually succeeded when Judah and his army of dissidents entered Jerusalem in triumph and ritually cleansed it of idol worship.

Our hike began in the Ben Shemen Forest, which is named for the plentiful olive trees growing here; *shemen* means "oil" in Hebrew. Some of the twisted trees were clearly centuries old, whereas others were recently planted in the land reclamation program. Like all the planted forests in Israel, Ben Shemen was orderly and pleasant, and included plaques giving the names of donors. Jeep roads crisscrossed the woods in the shadow of pine and cypress trees. We walked among pink, lavender, yellow, and white flowers scattered on the forest floor. Birds chirped in chorus, but we saw no other people.

We didn't expect to meet many people today. After all, if I had a free day and was looking for a hike, I wouldn't choose a route that paralleled Route 6. By our twenty-seventh day of hiking the

*Shvil*, we had only met one fellow through-hiker, Arnon, whom we met on our first day. Before we left home I had asked Danny, the Israel Trail coordinator, how many people hiked the length of the Trail yearly. He estimated the number to be a couple hundred and informed me that at this moment there were about fifty groups on the Trail. Accordingly, I had expected to meet an average of one group a day.

"Where are they all?" I asked John.

We thought it would be fun to meet other hikers coming toward us and ask them about the territory we were approaching, the trail conditions, and places to find food.

"Are you sure that's what he said?" asked John. "Maybe he was including groups who go out one day a month for years and stuff like that."

Anyway, we wondered how Danny knew who was or wasn't on the Trail. If I hadn't happened to call him, he wouldn't have known we were hiking.

We often discussed this as we walked along. John and I had been married for nearly thirty years and had always found something to talk about. But I was noticing that many of our conversations on the trail tended to repeat themselves.

After an hour's walk, we emerged from the forest on the top of Tel Hadid, where we had dramatic views in all directions—the Judean Hills behind us and the Mediterranean coast in front. The *tel*'s strategic importance was obvious; though not particularly high, it was the last hillside before the coastal plains. Archaeologists have determined that a town had existed in that place for 3500 years. Hadid is mentioned in the Bible as one of the cities to which the Israelites returned after the Babylonian exile.

Looking in the direction of Tel Aviv, we found it difficult to comprehend that we would be hiking through this densely populated area. Where was the Trail in the midst of all the concrete, asphalt, plaster, cinderblocks, and glass?

When we were hiking along trails in the desert regions I sometimes wondered how the Trail planners had decided on the Israel Trail route. Did they go up and down different *wadis* trying to find ones that connected and that led in the right direction? They must have studied the topographical maps and searched for interesting paths. Finding a way through this urban jungle would be no less challenging. I had the feeling we would be plunging into an unusual adventure.

When I returned home at the end of our journey I found a map of Israel produced especially for the *Shvil* and on it a short history of the Trail. I learned that the Committee for Israel's Trails, the Society for Protection of Nature in Israel, and the Israel Nature and Natural Parks Protection Authority cooperated in searching out the over ten-thousand kilometers of marked trails covering the width and breadth of the country. Their goal was to connect the best of the trails in this complicated system as a sort of Israel spinal cord.

We were walking close to what we call in Israel "the seam line," a term referring to the border separating Israel proper from the Palestinian Authority. This was the delineation between the 1967 borders of Israel and the West Bank territories captured in the Six-Day War. It's also called the Green Line. The name is derived from the green pen used to draw the border on the map of the armistice agreement with Jordan in 1949.

On some parts of our route today we would be only three kilometers from Palestinian villages. But as we walked most of the day through rolling hills, amidst shady forests, and in fields nestled in *wadis*, we could almost forget that we were just meters away from political turmoil and rushing traffic.

The red-tiled roofs of new Israeli settlements stood out between the Arab villages—two peoples living on the same land, each claiming ownership of it. Although perhaps most of them wished it weren't so, their lives were as intertwined as the branches on a grape vine. What is the solution to the Israeli/

Palestinian conflict? Where is justice? Many people feel that they have the answer. Especially people who come to Israel for a quick visit find the resolution to be very simple. But the longer we live here the more we become aware of the complications. We are thankful we aren't politicians; we've learned that no human system can bring about peace. God gave us peace in our hearts when we started to believe in Him, and we know that only He will bring peace to the world and to our own troubled part of it.

Geographically we were following another seam line, as we observed from the top of the *tel*. To the east, our right, were the rolling hills of Samaria; on the left, the Sharon coastal plain. The east was emptier and more undeveloped, to the west we saw quarries, *moshavim*, greenhouses, housing projects, and Ben Gurion International Airport.

The contrast between the ancient and modern, remarkable throughout Israel, was never more conspicuous than here in the center of the land. As we followed the trail through green rocky hillsides, we came upon exposed white bedrock indicating the ruins of a former settlement, including walls, cisterns, rooms, and an intricate mosaic floor. A dozen meters away traffic sped by at 120 kilometers an hour.

After descending steeply from Tel Hadid on a jeep trail, we were approaching Route 6, and according to the map, the trail crossed to the other side. I wondered how we'd get there.

"I'm not planning on risking my life and running across the highway again," I told John.

My question was answered when we descended an incline and passed through a long concrete drainage tunnel under the highway. Soon afterwards we found ourselves navigating an enormous new building project—an industrial park, we guessed. A vast area of land was torn up and hillsides were denuded. The heavy bulldozers, trucks and tractors made such a racket that we could barely hear one another's voice; even worse, the *Shvil* signs were gone.

I missed those quiet, happy days in the desert.

"Now what?" I asked John as I took out the map. The development was so new it wasn't marked on our map. The noise was grating on my nerves, and I could feel uneasiness growing in me.

John rose to the challenge. "We'll just bushwhack our way through and continue straight on till we find the Trail again," he said, helping me over a newly felled tree. "Take a picture and we'll remember this part of the *Shvil* too."

Gradually the din subsided behind us, and the stark brown cuts in the earth gave way to verdant hillsides dotted with my favorite anemones. In front of us, to my delight, a tri-colored logo appeared.

Overhead we saw white streaks crossing the sky, but thankfully we weren't close enough to hear the roar of the jets taking off and landing.

"Ben Gurion," John said. "We walked to the airport."

John's cell phone rang. In the desert we had no reception, and even in this area we had left the phone off much of the time. Most of our friends had learned not to call us.

"Hey Jim! What's happening?" John asked. "How are things in Eilat?"

"Everything's okay. Here's what I was thinking—I'm going to make a big party before I leave, and it'll also be a birthday party for you. A barbeque in the Shelter to say good-bye to everyone. You'll be here, won't you?"

"I'll talk it over with Judy." John closed the phone and turned to me. "Jim says everything's okay. And he has the idea of making a big party before he leaves, to say goodbye to everyone, and also to celebrate my birthday. A barbeque at the Shelter. He wants us to be there. We've got no choice," he said. "I don't need a birthday party—I'd rather spend my birthday with you on the *Shvil*. But after all Jim's done for us, coming from California to be here while we're gone, we'll have to go home for it."

John was right. We couldn't let Jim leave without saying good-bye. I don't know what I thought when we left; maybe I had simply tried not to think about it; Jim was already staying a week longer than he had planned.

"Will we be able to finish by then?" John asked.

According to my calculations, we would be someplace in the Galilee, maybe around Tiberius, with still about one-hundred kilometers to go. Then what? Go home and come back later to where we had left off? Or could we leave the hostel and congregation alone without Jim for another week or so?

"Let's try to walk faster and farther every day," John said.

Even as he spoke, John knew this was impossible. We couldn't speed up our walking pace, and our daily distance was usually determined by where roads intersect the Trail. We decided to simply continue our journey and fly home for the party. Once we were back in Eilat, we would decide whether we could return right away to the Trail.

"If not," said John, "we'll finish up next year."

"No!" I wanted to cry. Yet I had known from the start that many factors could keep us from fulfilling our goal. At the beginning I wasn't concentrating so much on reaching the end as on getting started and giving it a try. Now that we were about half way, I found it difficult to let go of our ultimate objective and just enjoy every day.

One benefit of hiking through the region of Sharon in the winter was that we were in the heart of Israel's citrus country. Skirting the periphery of several *kibbutzim* and *moshavim*, we passed along groves of luscious clementines and oranges. Their blossoms perfumed the air, and the fruit was ours for the picking as it was throughout Israel: God's welfare system.

"Remember, it is written in the Torah that farmers must leave some fruit on their trees for the poor, and not plow the corners of their fields," John said as he reached up to pick a perfect orange.

Starting out the first day with a group from The Shelter
(Judy fourth from right, and John on right)

The outside pages of the Hebrew tract that the Pexes gave to people they
met on the Trail. The title on left reads, "Stand and Walk the Land." The
other titles read, "A Dream Fulfilled" and "You're invited." The left lower
corner shows the Israel Trail logo.

Sunset at Nahal Raham

On top of Mt. Yahav

A cave for the night

The Carbolet ("Knife Edge")

Bedouin and sheep on the way up to Arad

Sheep grazing in the anemones

Steps up to Sataf, flanked by almond trees in blossom

Picking oranges

Approaching the Trans-Israel Highway
(Tel Aviv in background and Trail sign visible on rock)

First encounter with the Yarkon River

Emerging from the Yarkon in busy Tel Aviv

Crossing the Yarkon

Hiking up the coast

Walking through the Arab town of Jasr-a-Zarka
(Trail sign on electric pole)

Below the ancient city of Appolonia, with Racheli and Hadas (left)

Through the sabra (cactus) forest

A break while climbing Mt. Carmel

A break with friends near Nazareth, like Jesus and His disciples

John and Racheli lost in the mustard flowers

Storks in front of Mt. Tabor

Nahul Amad ("The Pillar")

John speaking with soldiers with heavy packs near the top of Mt. Meron

One of the many crossings of Nahal Dishon

Negotiating the trail around Nahal Snir

View of Mt. Hermon

On top of Mt. Hermon

Descending Mt. Hermon

The end of the Trail

Celebration meal for finishing the Trail!

And 30th wedding anniversary!

Tree-ripened in Israel's golden sunshine, the sweet fruit juices dripped down my chin and into John's beard.

Tel Afek, one of Israel's national parks, rose squarely above the flat wheat fields and orchards. In ancient times Afek was an important city along the trade and caravan route from Egypt to Damascus and Mesopotamia, and was the scene of some famous biblical battles. Its strategic location on a pass between the Yarkon River and the hills of Samaria, between the Philistines on the plains and the Israelites in the hills, placed it in the center of considerable action through the centuries.

In the time of King Saul, when the Philistines captured the Ark of the Covenant, 30,000 Israelite soldiers perished at Afek, including Eli, the high priest, and his two sons. More recently, only 2,000 years ago, king Herod built a new city here and called it Antipatris after the name of his father. The apostle Paul, under the protection of hundreds of soldiers, spent a night at Antipatris on his way from Jerusalem to Caesarea after having been arrested and falsely accused of defiling the Temple.

Shaded by trees and with abundant water, Afek was an ideal respite for weary travelers. We were near the springs that feed the Yarkon River. Though it is Israel's second-longest river after the Jordan, the Yarkon is notorious not for its length so much as for being Israel's filthiest river, the deposit for municipal sewage and industrial effluents from greater Tel Aviv. Though efforts are being made to purify it, and its source and end are now much cleaner, the middle stretch of the Yarkon is still polluted and definitely not recommended for swimming.

According to my Trail book, the route continued north from the source of the Yarkon toward Kfar Saba, a medium-sized, pleasant though nondescript city, and followed various highways—not the most picturesque setting. Furthermore, in some places it was next to the wall Israel built as protection from Palestinian suicide bombers. Again, not an especially scenic route. I was thankful to be on the new version of the *Shvil* that headed east toward the Mediterranean coast.

"They ought to come out with a new book already," I remarked to John. "This could be pretty confusing."

The current route led us through a tunnel under the highway and over a meandering path along the Yarkon. On the other side of the underpass our trail signs mysteriously disappeared.

"Look at the map, Jupe. The Trail must be around here someplace."

We met a man on a motorcycle and before we could open our mouths he asked, "Are you looking for the Israel Trail? You're very close. I have a forum on the Internet about the Trail. My name's Noam. Just look it up on tapuz.co.il. You can check it out sometime. Happy to meet you."

"Here's something we wrote about our walk," John offered.

"Thanks."

"What's a forum?" John asked me after Noam roared off.

"I'm not sure," I answered. "I don't do those things, but maybe I'll try to find his when we get home."

A few minutes later we encountered the Yarkon, its muddy green waters moving placidly towards the sea. Enormous eucalyptus trees bent over the stream. Stepping-stones in the river led us across to the other bank.

"So this is the famous Yarkon," John said.

"Or infamous," I added.

"It seems so pastoral here," continued John.

Along the Yarkon we felt as if we were in an undeveloped rural area, not near a great metropolis like Tel Aviv. Though in some places we were close to roads and could hear the distant roar of traffic, down in the streambed we could see only reeds, towering eucalyptus trees, glimpses of the river, and the sky

above us. At one point we caught sight of a *tel* rising above
the plowed brown fields, but as we drew closer we realized it
was an immense mountain of refuse accumulated from millions
of citizens. I had read about a plan to turn it into part of the
huge urban Ayalon Park. This complex environmental project will
include green spaces, bicycle routes and walking paths surrounding
"Garbage Mountain."

A grapefruit orchard abutting the trail beckoned us to pick the
fruit. The large brilliant globes looked too heavy to be supported
by the spindly branches. Around one of the countless twists in the
road we came upon a flock of white and black geese, paddling and
splashing in the water.

The Yarkon had overflowed its banks after recent heavy rains.
As we picked our way through a particularly miry section, we
came around a bend and saw three SUVs stuck in chocolate-
colored mud up to their axles. Three middle-aged men clothed
only in briefs were milling around nearby, scrutinizing their cars
from every angle.

*Why did they even try to drive through?* we wondered. The
two deep ruts in the road were filled with water. And after the
first vehicle became trapped in the sticky muck, why did the other
two follow him?

The new-model SUVs filled the entire breadth of the trail,
leaving us no room to pass, so we decided it was a good time for
a granola bar break and to sit back and watch the action—how they
would extricate themselves. We guessed they were businessmen
on their lunch hour, out for a spin on a back road and they had
stripped down to their briefs to prevent their suits from soiling.
Or perhaps they had been waiting weeks for a day off together.
In any case, they were now doubtless sorry they had started up
this impassable track.

The men must have seen us, but were so caught up in talking,
inspecting, and climbing in and out of the different jeeps, that they

paid no attention to two hikers leaning back against a tree.

We had seen enough of the movie. They weren't any closer to being freed than when we had stopped. John was convinced they needed a tractor to tow them out. We stood up.

"Shalom!" we said, approaching the first vehicle. In no mood for a friendly conversation, the men squeezed themselves against their cars, allowing us to pass.

"Who needs an SUV in places like this?" John remarked. We had long ago decided that walking was our preferred mode of transport.

After a short flat spell, the road dipped down into the river's bank and forded the Yarkon. We had no choice but to remove our shoes and socks, roll up our pants, and cross the stream.

"I hope it's not too cold or polluted," I said.

"We got all our shots last year when we went to Africa, so we're okay," answered John, one foot already in the water.

I waited for John to reach the other side before I dared to cross. But it was easier than I anticipated—the water wasn't higher than his knees, the current wasn't swift, and if I hadn't heard about the Yarkon's pollution, I would have never guessed.

A few minutes later we made it to the other side without mishap. Soon the trail took a sharp turn; we found ourselves on a sidewalk next to a crowded street in the heart of Tel Aviv, amidst the noise and exhaust of cars.

*How did we land here?* I thought. With our backpacks, muddy clothes and walking sticks, we felt like aliens from another planet. We followed trail signs on electricity poles, waited at a red light to cross the highway, and shortly the *Shvil* entered spacious Yarkon Park, a grassy expanse next to the river. Volleyball and basketball courts, soccer fields, picnic tables, and row boats completed the picture—a green oasis in a busy city.

*Tel Aviv is also part of Israel*, I thought, *so why shouldn't it be included in the Israel Trail?*

From what I had read and experienced of the 2175-mile Appalachian Trail, I decided that the *Shvil*, with its almost daily changes in geography, suited us better. Trekking days and weeks through deep woods and never crossing a road seemed boring to me compared to the variety we were experiencing.

A young woman in a short red skirt, tight blouse, and high heels was walking her dog in the park.

"Hi!" John greeted her. "We're on the Israel Trail, walked twenty-nine days from Eilat. I've got something for you to read."

*What would she care about the Trail?* I thought, and then was surprised at how friendly she was and how open to receive our tract.

At random points along the *Shvil* are placed large signs which include a map of that particular trail segment along with advice for hikers. Often the placards are set at trail or highway intersections. I love coming across them because they look so official, and it makes me feel that someone is looking out for us hikers. We certainly didn't expect to find a signboard next to the sidewalk in the Yarkon Park. How many people walking by here would be interested in the Israel Trail?

A couple with a baby in a stroller and an older couple were standing in front of the sign. We paused next to them.

"We're on the Trail, walked here from Eilat," John informed them.

"Wow, really?" the young father said. "What's it like? Where do you sleep? How far do you walk a day?"

"We're from England, visiting our children here," the older gentleman added. "We love hiking around England. Do you think we could manage the Israel Trail?"

We happily answered their questions, then shook hands as we parted ways.

The Trail followed the bank of the Yarkon almost to the point where it spilled into the Mediterranean Sea, and then with a sharp turn headed north. We were about to enter a new phase of the Trail—walking along the Mediterranean coast. On the way we would sleep with friends in Caesarea, the grandiose city founded by Herod the Great, and today the home of many of Israel's rich and famous.

Our daughter, Racheli, joined us again, this time together with her roommate, Hadas; they had a free day from their university studies. We arranged to meet them where the Trail passed the bus station in north Tel Aviv; we had to wait forty-five minutes for them. Whereas normally we find it difficult to be held up, this time we waited patiently. We hoped to remember this lesson after we finished our journey—not to lose our peace over small disappointments and setbacks. I wanted to keep my focus on the big picture—in this case on the end of the Trail. Naturally there would be hindrances and delays along the way, but with God's help we would finish and have the victory.

Racheli was apologetic when she stepped off the bus. "It took longer than we thought," she said.

She began demonstrating to Hadas her expertise in locating the Trail logos. The next two days we'd be walking on the coast, and already our sign-hunting skills were challenged on the sandy, wide Herzliya beach with few Trail signs.

"It doesn't matter," John insisted. "You can see there's only one way to go—up the coast."

"But we want to show Hadas how the *Shvil* works," I said, scanning the beach from the water's edge up to the dunes until I noticed the familiar stripes on the steps of the lifeguard's stand. We charged off in that direction.

Then for the first time since leaving home, I felt an ache in my right knee. After twenty-nine days of health and strength I was surprised to encounter that well-known twinge. Walking in the soft sand was obviously a strain; it was high tide and the sand was wet. Each step became an effort.

"How are your knees?" I asked John after a few minutes.

"I'm fine," answered John.

"Mine are hurting for some reason," I admitted. "Could I maybe borrow your braces?"

"Sure," John agreed. "I don't use them any more." We seemed to trade off with our aches and pains.

The beach ended and we were walking under cliffs. An ancient city, Apollonia, stood on the bluff above. Inhabited at various times by Phoenicians, Greeks, Romans, Muslims, and Crusaders, it is slowly tumbling onto the waterfront below as pounding waves wear away the land. In some places the coast is only a few meters wide, and we found ourselves clambering over ancient walls, pillars, and enormous hewn-stone blocks.

We stopped for an early lunch on the shell-covered beach between the cliff and the shallow tide pools. Gulls swept down from the rocks to snatch fish with fierce squawks.

"Would you girls like some coffee?" John asked, wanting to share with Hadas this special Trail experience. "There's plenty of driftwood lying around."

We gathered a few pieces of flotsam, but, accustomed to camping in the desert, we hadn't reckoned on wet wood.

"Nearly got it now," said John as he madly fanned the sputtering flame. "Just a little more toilet paper and blow!"

Hadas was impressed and wondered aloud why she didn't escape more often from her daily routine into nature.

The section of the trail on top of the cliff provided striking views of the foamy white breakers below, as well as far up and down the coast. The path held fast to the edge.

"Reminds me of the *Carbolet*. Now that's something you should do someday," he advised the girls.

"But we're not on a knife-edge here, so it's not so scary," I added with my usual desire for accuracy. I remembered well the *Carbolet*'s steep drops on both sides of a narrow path.

Up on the bluff we passed through fields of grass and multi-colored flowers, but the most spectacular flower show awaited us at the Purple Iris Reserve near Netanya, Israel's largest city between Tel Aviv and Haifa. Clumps of enormous plum-colored irises grew in the sand between other beach-friendly bushes. We dashed from one cluster to the next.

"Over here, Jupe, get a picture of this one," John directed, "with the girls in front."

From the Iris Reserve, we entered the city of Netanya, a popular tourist destination with attractive, well-maintained beaches and a newly-renovated promenade. Trekking along it, I doubted that many people strolling on the boardwalk would notice the decorative white, blue, and orange stripes painted on the rubbish bins, and if they did, they would have no idea that they were walking on a bit of the Israel Trail.

Racheli and Hadas took the train back home to Rehovot. John and I enjoyed a tasty meal, a special visit, and good night's sleep at the home of our friends, Herbby and Anne, before setting out on our second coastal day.


The Trail descended again onto the beach north of Netanya. It seemed half the city's population was out for an early morning jog, walk, or run. At the end of the broad beach the ground under the cliffs was strewn with plastic bottles, throw-away plates and cups, broken glass, all sorts of garbage. *Was this Israel's contribution to the environment*, I wondered, knowing Israel's standards of outdoor cleanliness have much room for improvement, *or did it arrive here by sea from other countries in the Mediterranean basin? Perhaps some of the many unemployed could be put to work cleaning our beaches.*

When my stomach told me it was time for lunch, we found a spot under eucalyptus trees near a swamp, a paradise for water birds. We had just spread out on the ground our feast of cheese sandwiches and fruit when a car pulled up next to us on the dirt road.

"Are you on the Israel Trail?" the driver, a middle-aged man with a *kippa* on his head, inquired.

"Yes," John replied, not knowing why he asked. "It's our thirtieth day."

He smiled knowingly. "I think I met you near Eilat, on top of Har Amir, about a month ago."

John and I looked at each other and tried to think. "Hey, were you with that *yeshiva* group?" I suddenly remembered.

It had been our second day on the trail and we were exhausted after finally reaching the top of the mountain. A group of religious high school boys with their teachers had arrived from the other side of the hill and were also resting. Two of the students became excited when they heard we were on the *Shvil*, and taking out their little gas stove, they prepared a cup of sage tea for us.

How amazing! Not only that our paths would cross again, but that he would recognize us.

John handed him one of our pamphlets. "Here's something we wrote about our walk."

"Well done!" he said. "Keep it up!"

We waved good-bye as if to an old friend.

The Trail took us through a grassy park-like area studded with majestic spreading oak trees. Farther along, orange groves graced both sides of the dirt road.

"Let's pick some for Eunice," suggested John. "Everyone likes tree-ripened fruit." We would be staying that night with Eunice and Daniel, friends from Singapore.

After the orange trees, we walked through a eucalyptus forest, planted years ago in long straight rows, and then crossed the four-lane coastal highway on a pedestrian bridge.

A young man with a *kippa* stopped us in the middle of the overpass. "Are you on the Israel Trail?" he asked.

Smiling, John answered, "Yeah, our thirtieth day since leaving Eilat."

"Wow, that's my dream."

"Here, take this pamphlet we wrote, and visit us in Eilat."

As we approached Caesarea National Park, a large, brown, furry animal with a long tail scurried across our path. At one time we believed these were otters, but later learned they were mongoose. We were excited because, except for some ibex in the desert and a group of gazelles who appeared to be dancing in a circle in a field near Modi'in, we'd seen little wildlife on our hike.

Eunice met us at the Caesarea Amphitheater. In her gated community just north of the archaeological ruins, every house looked like a mansion. I didn't imagine that many Israel Trail hikers lodged in such luxury. It seemed that the town's developers were trying to compete with the monumental city built two thousand years ago by Herod the Great. Besides the amphitheater (which continues to be used for plays and concerts) the ancient city included an oil-fueled lighthouse, an advanced sewage system, a palace dedicated to Caesar, a theater, a hippodrome, and an aqueduct.

The aroma of Chinese food greeted us as we entered the Ongs' home. Soon we were seated at their round table feasting on a six-course meal, including a Peking duck that Daniel, Eunice's husband, had carried back in his hand luggage from his last business trip to Singapore.

"Can you believe we are on the *Shvil*?" I asked John as we lay in our king-sized bed that night.

"Why not?" John answered, and quickly fell asleep.

I wrote in my diary:

- *If I have a small problem on my feet—take care of it immediately (blister, thorn, piece of rock).*
- *A problem like a blister can come any time. Even though we've walked many days, we're not immune.*

I had felt a sharp pain under my foot earlier in the day, but hadn't wanted to stop and take off my boot. Finally, when I was beginning to limp, I told John I had to sit down for a minute. I turned my boot upside down and a tiny pebble fell out. I reflected that it's often the small things in life that irritate and disturb us. If I had taken the time to remove the pebble when I first felt it—to address the problem early—I would have saved myself hours of pain.

# 12. Elijah Country

"Hey! Today we'll climb the Carmel," John announced the next morning. Eunice and Daniel had just waved us off.

The Carmel was another milestone on our journey, and just the sight of its rise on the horizon inspired me. Reaching the Carmel meant that the desert, the center of the country, and the Mediterranean coast were all behind us. I wondered if by crossing this famous ridge, apparently a favorite place of the prophet Elijah, we would gain insight into the life of that eccentric, intense prophet.

"How are we doing for time?" John asked. "Think we'll finish before Jim goes home?"

"Looks to me like we'll be five or six days short."

I had been making calculations daily. "In Haifa we'll pick up the last maps, and then I can better estimate." We had given four maps and a stack of our tracts to our son, Josh, who studied in Haifa University.

As we plodded along Caesarea's sandy beach next to the ancient stone arches of the Roman aqueduct, John declared, "Jupe, do you realize we hiked the same route as the apostle Peter—from Jaffa to Caesarea?"

"Yeah, that's right. How long did it take him?"

"Two days, same as us. Peter must have been pretty excited as he walked with Cornelius' messengers. I'm sure he realized he

172

was starting something new, but he probably never imagined all the implications."

Peter and the rest of Jesus' disciples had been sharing the good news exclusively with the Jews, because the Jews believed in one God, possessed the Scriptures, and were waiting for their Messiah. In those days Jews didn't even associate with Gentiles, whom they believed to be unclean. Then Peter had a vision while praying on a rooftop in Jaffa (part of Tel Aviv today, but previously a major port), and he went to the Roman centurion Cornelius' home in Caesarea, opening the door for Gentiles to hear the message of God's love. Our fellowship in Eilat is an example that today God's family is composed of people from all nations and languages.

As I had these thoughts, an older gentleman with a cane, and his dog, approached. "Are you on the Israel Trail?" he asked.

"Our thirtieth day since Taba," John replied.

The inscription on the man's T-shirt read, *The International Four Days March, Nijmegen.*

"Have you been there?" I asked, pointing at the shirt.

"Yes," he answered. "I've been many times to Holland for the Four Days March, where I was one of over 35,000 participants. It's quite an experience."

"Hey, maybe that's something for us, Jupe." John was enthusiastic these days about any walking opportunity.

"Can you really see yourself walking with 35,000 other people?" I asked.

The man's name was Yonatan. He told us he had been a pilot on the Tel Aviv to Eilat route. In his free time he liked to hike. We were impressed to hear that he had spent two weeks on the Appalachian Trail. The previous year he fell while walking a stretch of the Israel Trail in the Galilee, sustained a multiple fracture in his leg, and was told his walking days were over. Unwilling to surrender, he was gradually building his strength through daily beach walks with dog and cane.

North of Caesarea we turned into Nahal Taninim, which means "Alligator Stream." Although we didn't see any alligators, the last one having been killed here about one hundred years ago, we saw many young Arab men fishing with nets. John approached one group of fishermen.

"We're on the Israel Trail. You should try it." They were happy to talk, but somehow I couldn't imagine these men on the *Shvil*. It's not for everybody.

"Come visit us in Eilat." John gave them a tract, and they wished us well.

As we traveled up the beach we were regularly crossing rivers which we hadn't been aware of before. Who hasn't heard of the "mighty and wide" Jordan River? The Jordan flows from north to south through the Rift Valley, from the Sea of Galilee to the Dead Sea. But Israel also has many shorter coastal rivers that originate in the hills and trickle out into the Mediterranean Sea. I say "trickle out," because with few exceptions, Israel's rivers are drying up. The water flow is dwindling as the water is diverted for agricultural purposes, and the remaining water is usually terribly polluted. Walking the Israel Trail made us aware of the existence of these rivers. We had crossed bridges without noticing the streams beneath them while zooming up the coastal highway in our car.

Now, after following the Yarkon River from its source to the sea, we waded across Nahal Poleg, walked several kilometers through reeds and eucalyptus trees along the winding Nahal Alexander, and rolled our pants above our knees to ford Nahal Hadera. At the banks of its muddy green waters, a large sign read: *The waters of the stream are polluted. It is strictly forbidden to swim.* We hesitated a moment, then waded across.

In a few hundred meters Nahal Taninim led us to Jasr-A-Zarka, an Arab city that contrasts with its prosperous southerly neighbor, Caesarea. On the outskirts of town, ramshackle huts stand on the beach, with dogs lying in the shade of fishing nets draped on poles. We weren't sure whether these were permanent homes or fishermen's cabins. Despite—or perhaps because of—the small settlement's air of neglect, it has the peculiar charm of fishing villages all over the world.

In the run-down center of town people were friendly and open to conversation. In front of a hole-in-the-wall store a few people stood around. One young man was on crutches.

John addressed him. "Hey, how's it going? We're on the Israel Trail. Can you read Hebrew? I'd like to give you something that we wrote."

In Israel people rarely refuse to accept a pamphlet or book, and this man was no exception.

He smiled. We said, "All the best!" as we strode off.

Trail signs on electricity poles guided us through narrow potholed streets and out the other side of town, where we got lost in a wheat field.

"At least we know which direction to go." John was bushwhacking through brambles. "We head for the Carmel Ridge. Here, Jupe, let me help you over this wall."

The stone wall, overgrown with grass, flowers, and bushes, turned out to be an extension of the Roman aqueduct. Moments like these—hiking along a two-thousand-year-old aqueduct complete with arches and an inscription from its builders, the Tenth Legion, minutes after walking through the streets of an Arab town—make the Israel Trail a unique experience.

We discovered the Trail sign painted on the aqueduct and followed the ancient water channel through a *moshav*. A *moshavnik* (member of a cooperative village) was working in his yard, and we asked if we could fill up our water bottles.

"Are you going skiing?" he asked.

"Sure, eventually," John said. "We're on the Israel Trail, thirty-one days since leaving Eilat, and we're headed for Mt. Hermon."

We were standing next to a *Shvil* marker painted on a pole stuck into the ground opposite his house.

"What's the Israel Trail?" he asked.

I'd become used to a general ignorance about the Trail. Some people called it in Hebrew the "Cross Israel," making it sound like one of the highways that cut across the land from north to south or east to west.

*Hadn't he seen any other grubby people with big backpacks walking by his gate?* I wondered. Then I answered. "It's a hiking trail, 940 kilometers from Eilat to Dan. A couple hundred people hike the whole thing every year."

We thanked him for the water, then followed Nahal Taninim through the vineyards for which this area was famous. We came to a modern-day aqueduct, a water pipeline crossing the stream. The *Shvil* logo was painted on it, four meters above the ground.

My heart beat wildly. *What? Me shimmy over that?*

John gave it a glance and quickly descended the creek's bank under the conduit. Only then did I notice the low water level and the stepping stones leading across the *wadi*. I was thankful we weren't here when the stream was flooded.

Soon we were heading up the "nose of the Carmel," as the southern tip of the Carmel Range is called. The Carmel Ridge, Israel's only mountainous outcrop into the sea along an otherwise smooth coastline, has been described as a big "bump" on the northern coast. The ridge rises gradually from the south, reaching elevations of over five-hundred meters above Haifa. Carmel in Hebrew means "God's vineyard" and symbolizes beauty in the Bible. In the Song of Songs in the Old Testament, the bridegroom exclaims that his lover's head "crowns you like Mt. Carmel."

Climbing again after walking along the coast for two days, I could feel the muscles in my legs straining. I needed a break; we had been walking a few hours already.

"Let's stop in this grove of oak trees," I suggested.

John was wary. "What about the cows?" Barbed wire fences here and there contained the free-ranging milk cattle.

"What about them? They're just cows." I settled onto a boulder amidst green shrubs and wildflowers.

We pulled out a couple of granola bars and apples, but John couldn't shake off his uneasiness. When a cow came up behind us mooing loudly, John grabbed his pole and assumed the stance of a gallant knight. The cow ambled on, oblivious.

At the top of the "nose" we came to a well-preserved archaeological site with stone arches and an ancient winepress. I found it interesting that wine has been produced here (in the heart of Israel's wine country) for two thousand years.

From behind the ruins came shouts of children. Surprised, we rounded the corner and found a school class sitting under a stately oak tree. Farther along the wide path we saw other school groups; then we understood we had reached a popular attraction. We had come to Ramat Hanadiv, the burial place of Baron Edmond de Rothschild and his wife. Baron Edmond began to buy land in Palestine in the 1880s and helped found Israel's wine industry. His tomb is in a crypt in the middle of beautiful gardens surrounded by a park that includes walking paths and archeological sites.

At the heart of the recreational area were grassy fields, picnic tables, barbeque pits, water faucets, and parking lots with rows of buses. The snack kiosk caught our attention. Before we started our hike, I had imagined us trekking all day, eating simple lunches of pita and peanut butter, munching on granola bars, but finding snack bars along the way where we could treat ourselves to an ice cream cone, soft drink, or candy bar. In the past we had often seen ice cream trucks parked at the end of popular trails. Perhaps because we were hiking in the off season and not on weekends, we had yet to encounter one of these vans; the subject of the ephemeral ice cream trucks was a recurrent topic of our conversations. Finally at Ramat Hanadiv I indulged my fantasy and ordered a chocolate-covered ice cream bar studded with sugary nuts.

The area was so well-organized with paths, arrows, signs, and trails, that we lost our *Shvil* markers. We located the information desk, and while speaking to the guide, we stood next to a man who turned around and asked, "Aren't you walking the Israel Trail? I saw you at the Shizafon junction." We had passed Shizafon on our fourth day out of Eilat.

The man's name was Ami. He told us he was a tour guide and was also hiking the *Shvil*, but he was doing it one week per month. Small world.

After the park we followed a jeep trail along the ridge through forests and scrublands. By 4 P.M., after eight hours on the trail, our pace had deteriorated to a robotic shuffle, but we still had to reach the *kibbutz* where we would spend the night with friends.

"I've gotta rest. I need an energy bar," I told John as I collapsed on the ground.

We sprawled on the dirt road, leaning against our packs. John closed his eyes and was snoring lightly when a young man with a large backpack came striding rapidly towards us from the opposite direction.

John quickly sat straight up and tilted back his head. "Shalom! Are you on the *Shvil?*"

Amit, the hiker, told us he had started in Eilat, stopped walking at the Large Crater, and had begun again nine days ago in the north.

Finally, on our thirty-first day, a fellow hiker. We could share information, exchange ideas, trade experiences. Amit didn't sit down.

"How many hours do you walk a day?" I asked.

"All day."

"What?! From six to six?"

"From seven till dark," he replied, taking off again.

"Strange," I said to John. "We look for every chance to stop and talk to people we meet. You'd think he'd be lonely walking alone day after day."

"Boy, that wouldn't be for me. Hike without you? Forget it." John stood and pulled me to my feet. I felt stronger after my energy bar and apple.

After an attempt at hitchhiking that ended up as a tedious tramp out to the highway and another attempt that ended in a bus ride, we finally reached the *kibbutz* at 6 P.M., where we were guests of Shira and Itai.

Although we had never considered becoming members, John and I always have enjoyed visiting *kibbutzim*; we both spent time there in the 1970s. Up until the 1980s each *kibbutz* had dozens of volunteers from all over the world, young people who were attracted to the opportunity of experiencing one of the largest communal movements in history.

The first *kibbutzim* were founded in the early 1900s as a response to the social, economic, and political realities of the time. Idealistic pioneers arriving in Palestine from Russia sought a connection to their ancestral land through agriculture, and they discovered that living communally was the most secure way to live in lawless and hostile surroundings. Their socialist ideology led the *kibbutzim* into a unique social experiment that attracted the attention of the whole world. Their aim was pure communism, and up until the 1970s the principle of equality was taken extremely seriously.

Gradually, however, cracks began to appear in the system. Even with the highest ideals, human nature does not conform to the model of collectivism. The *kibbutzniks* were no longer content to share every gift they received with all the other members, to raise their children in "children's houses," and to support lazy people who didn't contribute their share of labor. Around the time of the fall of the Iron Curtain and as the Chinese people were developing a passion for materialism, *kibbutzniks* were realizing that they couldn't construct a utopia here on earth, a perfect system where all people are equal. Built into the human being is the desire to receive recompense for his work and to be treated as an individual. Today most of the former collective communities resemble other villages, in that the residents have differential salaries, private cars, and eat in their own homes rather than in a communal dining room. Each time we visit *kibbutzim*, we are curious to observe the changes.

According to the map, the first three kilometers of our second day on the Carmel would follow a path on the ridge parallel to the highway. I envisioned a straightforward trail with views over the shining Mediterranean Sea.

"An hour should get us to Ein Hod," I guessed. "After that we have a long climb to the summit of the Carmel." Ein Hod is an artists' village, and I pictured a relaxing break with a cup of cappuccino and a piece of cheesecake at a charming coffee shop near the town's entrance.

The reality was totally different—a poorly-marked, ankle-twisting trail, with countless rocks, briars, and bristles. I was reminded of the curse God placed on Adam after his sin: "Cursed is the ground because of you ... it will produce thorns and thistles for you."

Needless to say, we met no hikers on this section. Anyone who knew better would never choose this path. Rather than leading us below through the pleasant banana plantations, their wide serrated leaves providing abundant shade, the trail continued along the edge of the stony hill.

"Whoever planned this path?" John was frustrated. Had someone with a few cans of paint randomly swabbed *Shvil* stripes here and there on stones? Up and down the hill we went, zigzagging back and forth, constantly extricating ourselves from the prickly thickets. Rather than admiring the stunning views, we were perpetually scanning the hillside for the obscure, disjointed Trail signs.

As if the boulders and spiky scrub bushes weren't enough, the Trail wended through several *sabra* (prickly pear) forests. The cacti's large, flat, olive-green pads possess needle-like thorns, while the prickles of the fist-sized orange fruits are so tiny they are impossible to remove from one's skin. We had to carefully thread our way through the sprawling cacti as through a dangerous maze.

*Sabra* is the word for the cactus fruit itself, and it's also used to refer to a native-born Israeli. According to the stereotype, the Israeli, like the prickly pear, is tough and thorny on the exterior but sweet and soft inside.

After three hours of walking we arrived at the entrance to Ein Hod, my cozy café nowhere in sight. We could have hiked up the steep hill into the center of town, but we were already running late and had no energy for extra kilometers.

"Never mind." John tried to console me. "Remember when we drove through here last summer and we stopped to buy some Druze pita at the next intersection?" The flat *pitot* the Druze produce are paper thin and as large as tires.

"You think the stand'll still be there?" I tried to conceal my disappointment. It wasn't what I'd had in mind.

"Why wouldn't it?" John evidently hadn't shared my fixation on the café, but he adored Druze pita.

We passed the Etzba ("finger") Cave on our descent to the picnic area where we had planned to have lunch. With its stalagmites, stalactites, and bats, the cave would be worth taking some extra time to explore. However, as we circled around large boulders and faced the cavern's gaping entrance we were faced with a class of thirty second-grade boys. Their teachers' long

beards, head coverings, black pants, and white shirts indicated that
they were from a very religious stream of education. We quickly
understood that unless we were willing to wait, we would have
to forego our excursion into the cave. While one of the teachers
was lecturing the boys, a young man on the edge of the group
turned towards us.

"Are you going skiing?" he asked.

"We're on the *Shvil Israel*," John replied, immediately forgetting the stalagmites and bats. "Our thirty-second day from Eilat."

"How much water do you carry? Where do you sleep?"

John answered his questions, and we found him to be unusually friendly. I was surprised that he'd even heard of the Trail and
had asked intelligent questions.

"Here's something for you to read. It explains our journey,"
John offered.

We had met many religious people on our walk, but I still
wasn't used to sharing our faith with them. As we headed down the
hill I glanced back and saw our young friend, Azariah, handing our
pamphlet to the older rabbi.

*That's the end of it*, I thought. *I wish he would've at least read
what we wrote before the rabbi rips it up.*

John's stand selling Druze pita turned out to be as elusive
as my coffee shop. So we contented ourselves with our packed
lunch and a rest before the long ascent up the Carmel. When
the religious boys reached the picnic area, Azariah came running
over to us.

"He's probably furious. Maybe his rabbi read our tract and
found out we believe in Jesus," I braced myself for his outburst.

Azariah pulled the tract out of his shirt pocket.

"He still has it." I was amazed.

"Is this your address on the back?" he asked. "If I come to
Eilat, could you give me ideas about walking the Trail?"

"Sure," John replied. "Anytime."

The climb up to the five-hundred-meter summit of the Carmel was a cross-section of typical Mediterranean scrub forest: carobs, oaks, pines, and laurels, with a tangled thicket underneath. I gained a new respect for Elijah. How did he maneuver through the brush with no maps or guidebooks? Didn't he find himself exhausted sometimes?

But Elijah was a man with a mission, not out on a pleasure walk. He came to the Carmel to challenge the priests of the Canaanite god Baal to a contest designed to reveal the one true God. A person who feels himself directed by God is able to overcome all sorts of obstacles.

The ungodly king of Israel, Ahab, went to meet Elijah and was furious with him after three years of drought. Elijah ordered Ahab to summon the people, including the 450 prophets of Baal and 400 prophets of Asherah, to a meeting on Mt. Carmel. Ahab's ready compliance to the order of this roughshod prophet shows the dominance of Elijah's personality.

"I wonder why Elijah chose the Carmel to confront Ahab," I said. It was far from his home in Gilead (present-day Jordan).

Did Elijah reckon that Ahab would be more prone to agree to an assembly on his own territory? Mt. Carmel, at one time the location of an altar of the Lord, had apparently become a favorite site for Baal worship.

"I picture Elijah as a kind of rough mountain-man, a bony Bedouin, walking all over the place, from Lebanon to Mt. Sinai," said John. "He probably didn't have much to eat. But what a man of God!"

The lengthy ascent of the Carmel offered lush forests, natural caves, hidden valleys, and the first rock climbing we had encountered since the Negev. The Israel Trail crossed the road not far from the traditional site of Elijah's showdown and victory over the false prophets. To our surprise, we were only minutes from the house of our friends, John and Ruth. After ten hours on the trail we collapsed into their comfortable armchairs and enjoyed cold glasses of lemonade.

The following day, we were delighted to have our daughter, Racheli, join us for the third time. On the well-traveled route down the other side of the Carmel Ridge, people we met asked why we were hiking from south to north rather than from north to south.

"Why did you choose to hike uphill?" people asked.

Evidently they looked at the map and concluded that hiking south would be like rolling downhill. I explained that we began in Eilat at sea level and would end in *Kibbutz* Dan at two hundred meters above sea level. In a trek of over nine hundred kilometers the ascent was insignificant. But many people still didn't grasp it. Here on the Carmel Ridge was one place where it would certainly have been easier to come from the other direction.

The bottom of the hill brought us to Kibbutz Yagur, one of Israel's largest *kibbutzim*. As early as the 1960s the *kibbutzim* had launched into manufacturing and most had small factories of plastic, rubber, food, or metal. Today they are developing tourism, shopping malls, gas stations, and banquet halls. Kibbutz Yagur is known for its riding club. As we walked along the edge of the *kibbutz*, John noticed a toilet inside the fence and decided to take advantage of it.

A *kibbutznik* rode by on a tractor. "That toilet's private," he said coldly. "It's not for walkers. I have to clean it."

Racheli and I exchanged glances. *What now?* I wondered.

John responded quickly with a smile. "We're on the Israel Trail, day thirty-three since leaving Eilat. I invite you to our hostel in Eilat, the first night for free! Do you remember Ben?"

The tractor driver's face lit up. "Ben? Sure. Great kid. He used to ride here and work with us."

"We're in touch with his family in the States," John continued. "They hope to come back."

"Give Ben regards from Iftach. We hope to see him soon."

"Okay, and we hope to see you in Eilat!" John said. "Here's a paper we wrote about our journey."

"Thanks. Shalom, shalom!" Iftach waved as he drove off on his tractor.

After he left, John, Racheli and I each took a turn using the toilet.

On the other side of the highway from Kibbutz Yagur was Kfar Hassidim, a religious agricultural village founded eighty years ago by *Hassidim* (a sect of Orthodox Jews who follow a strict interpretation of the Mosaic Law) from Poland. As the trail led down the main street of the settlement, we felt conspicuous; all the women wore ankle-length skirts and long-sleeved blouses and all the men had on long pants and *kippot*.

A man on a tractor pulled into a driveway ahead of us and called out, "Shalom! I want to show you something."

We looked around, not sure he was speaking to us. "Yes, come here. My name is Gadi Jakob," he said, jumping off his tractor and approaching us with outstretched hand.

*This should be interesting*, I thought. We didn't have a strenuous hike that day, so we had time to visit.

Gadi, a man about our age with a large colorful *kippa* on his head and a handlebar mustache, led us to what looked like a small barn alongside his house. When he opened the door and turned on the light we realized we hadn't entered a barn, but a museum. A long sturdy wooden table and chairs took up the center of the room, and shelves lining the walls were jam-packed with artifacts.

"I'm sure you'll drink a cup of tea," he said. "I have pastries and almonds, the traditional food we offer as a blessing to guests."

Gadi, who said he used to travel around the former Soviet

Union for his work, had collected old tools, toys, musical instruments, clocks, lamps, anything connected to life in the *shtetl* (a Jewish village in pre-Holocaust Europe) in the nineteenth century. Gradually Gadi became an expert on that era. My interest was aroused because both my father's and mother's families had come from a similar background.

Two years before, a personal tragedy had spurred Gadi to deepen his involvement: his son was killed in a skirmish with terrorists. Gadi's museum provided an outlet for his sorrow.

Not anxious for us to leave, Gadi demonstrated for us his wooden toys, inviting Racheli to try a game requiring her to pop a ball on a string through a circular hole in a ruler-sized piece of wood. He played soulful accordion music on an old gramophone, and insisted that Racheli squat over a traditional chamber pot. Finally he showed us his detailed plans to develop a tourist village in which people could experience life in the *shtetl* including artisan's workshops, restaurants, gift shops, and an inn.

We finally had to pull ourselves away from this extraordinary man. I hoped his dream would become a reality and that in the future we would see his *shtetl* rising out of the present corn fields.

"We won't be needing lunch for a while now," I said to Racheli after we shook Gadi's hand and wished him well.

"Take a picture, Jupe," John said.

That afternoon the trail meandered up and down hills, through lost valleys and miniature wheat fields curving in the hollows between ridges. The tree-covered ranges looked like a neo-impressionist painting in the pointillism style—millions of dots of varying shades of green. Birds serenaded us, but except for a few shepherds, we met no people.

We lost the trail markers for a time in the waist-high tracts of mustard flowers. But this time even I wasn't anxious. Steep hills rose on both sides of the narrow valley, so obviously we were meant to follow the flower-filled *wadi*.

Just as we stumbled upon the *Shvil* logo again, two young men in sandals, with scrubby beards and bulky backpacks came striding toward us. Although the only through-hikers we had encountered so far were Arnon on our first day and the brisk young man two days previously, we instantly recognized these guys as the real thing.

"Are you on the *Shvil*?" John asked.

"Yes!" they answered, stopping in their tracks. "We began at Dan 10 days ago. Do you have time to stop?"

Our kind of people. "Sure, why not?"

Here, under an oak tree amid fragrant flowers was a perfect place for a break. They introduced themselves as Gil and Oded and produced a gas cook stove from one of their packs. "How about a cup of coffee?"

I made a quick mental calculation that now we wouldn't reach the junction I had aimed for, but who cared? There was another intersection a few kilometers closer. Oded and Gil said they were taking it easy on the Trail, stopping whenever anything caught their interest. We found we had a lot to talk about. They had recently finished the army and said that planning this trip had helped them to endure its trials. They told us they were carrying twenty-five kilos.

"How do you do it in sandals?" I asked.

Gil replied, "After three years of heavy army boots, I want my feet free. But I'm carrying hiking boots just in case."

"Take a picture of the four of us, Racheli," John said.

We gave them our tract and phone number, and offered to help them with water in the south. It happened that we later picked them up when they left the trail and hitchhiked for provisions, and we met again just as they were finishing the *Shvil* in Eilat. By the third time, we felt like best friends.

Farther on we passed two ancient, abandoned flour mills. Until the 1940s the mills used the traditional system of millstones turned by water from the stream. One of them was called "The Monks' Mill" because it was built in the nineteenth century by monks from the Carmelite Monastery. When they eventually weren't able to compete with modern mills, the place was abandoned. Then recently, young people converted its old stone buildings into a sort of hostel.

We approached it over a narrow arched bridge which spanned the rapidly flowing stream. Donkeys brayed and chickens cackled in the enclosed yard.

We finished our day in an Arab village where Jonathan, the son of the friends we'd stayed with the previous night, was waiting for us in his car.

"You asked if we wanted to hike with you tomorrow," Jonathan said. "We've decided to take up your offer. I have a few free days from the army. Looks like there'll be five of us—my brother Dave, his friend Eli, Karen, and Hanan."

"Great!" I said, wondering how it would be to hike with someone currently in the pilots' course, the most rigorous of army training. At least Hanan, who was our age, would be with us so Jonathan and his friends couldn't push us too hard.

Later that evening when we were alone I reminded John, "Another week till your birthday."

"Yeah, I can't believe I'll be fifty-nine."

"Strange to think we'll be home in Eilat then."

I wondered if we'd return to finish our journey.

# 13. In the Footsteps of Jesus

I found out how different it is to hike with a group. We had the logistics of driving in two cars to our end point, parking Hanan's car there, and afterwards driving the other car back to the *kibbutz* where we began our hike. And I soon found that a large band of people travel more slowly than a couple, even though they're all in excellent shape. On the other hand, we got to share our *Shvil* experience with friends and enjoy stimulating conversation.

"Do you mind if I hold the map?" Dave asked. He had been a sports instructor in the army and had experience navigating. "I'll carry your pack too."

"And then let me have a turn," Eli insisted.

I felt sorry for John. Every time we hiked with others, even with Racheli, I was relieved of my pack. But perhaps people considered it unmanly for a man not to carry his own backpack. On second thought, I didn't think John minded.

When we began our trek, I had kept our map handy in the outside pocket of my pack and I'd ask John to take it out when I wanted to check our position, until I discovered John's frequent noncompliance with my requests. So I transferred the map to John's outside pocket where I could access it freely—when I could convince him to stop long enough.

"Again?" he would protest.

Now Dave strode along with the map grasped in his hand in front of his face, so that he could refer to it constantly. I felt like a Cub Scout in the presence of an Eagle Scout. I also felt vindicated before John. After observing Dave's technique, he couldn't be so quick to say, "Again?" to me when I asked to look at the map. In fact, I resolved to refer to it more often.

We hiked through hills and valleys in the vicinity of Nazareth. Huge olive trees studded the landscape, their trunks gnarled and twisted with age. How long had these trees been around? Since the time of Jesus? The *Shvil* often used pre-existing trails. Could it be that Jesus had walked these same paths with His disciples? We were close to His hometown.

In a grassy field under the shade of sweeping oak trees, we stopped for a snack and a rest. Thrilled to be traveling with us, Hanan prayed for the Lord to bless our sandwiches and fruit. As we lifted our voices in Hebrew worship songs, I could imagine Jesus passing through this area with His disciples, singing and talking as they went along. They must have paused as we did to share a few *pitot* together.

Three hours of hiking brought us to the edge of Tzipori, a *moshav* on the site of an ancient Galilean town. As is common in Israel, it was at various times a Jewish, Roman, Arab, Byzantine, and Crusader settlement. At its prime in the first century A.D., Tzipori was "the glory of the Galilee" and was the most important city in Israel after Jerusalem. According to tradition, Mary, the mother of Jesus, was born in Tzipori. Ruins have been uncovered indicating that Messianic Jews lived here alongside religious Jews.

"What d'you think about visiting the Ellises?" asked Dave.

"I guess we've got the time," I agreed. "And their house isn't far off the path."

Tal and Adi Ellis, friends of ours, raise goats, and recently opened a small restaurant and shop featuring the cheeses that Tal has developed. Although we were not expected, they immediately ushered us into their airy, artistically-decorated shop and placed before us an attractive and tasty platter with a sampling of their gourmet cheeses. After nearly an hour, we could barely pull ourselves away from the comfortable atmosphere, but the Trail was waiting.

Almost immediately after that we got lost. One minute we were all in a group following the Trail logos painted on rocks, and a few minutes later there was no logo to be found, and we were scattered all over the hillside searching for one. Jonathan went down the hill with the map. Hanan, Karen, and Dave went up the hill to where they thought the Trail would eventually emerge. John decided we should go back several hundred meters and around several bends to where we remembered seeing the last sign. Eli stuck with us.

After much searching, Eli found a marker and was trying to determine in which direction it pointed, when he received a call on his cell phone from Dave whose group had taken a short-cut and found the signs farther on.

When we all located each other again, we were standing in front of the tomb of Rabbi Yehuda Hanasi.

"When John and I get lost," I explained, "we just go back to the last sign."

"That's the way to do it," Dave agreed. "That's how we learned in our navigating course."

*At least we were doing something right*, I thought.

In Israel, many graves of rabbis—and of their children, and sometimes their wives—have been turned into shrines and places of pilgrimage. Most of the graves date from the time of the Talmud, two thousand years ago. The faithful who flock to these holy places believe they will receive a blessing, although rabbinic opinions vary regarding the benefit of praying at the graves of the righteous. Traditionally, making requests of the dead is prohibited in Judaism, but religious leaders tend to explain these pilgrimages as a source of inspiration from the holy person or as a request that the good works of the deceased rabbi be added to one's own deeds.

North African and Hassidic Jews particularly seek out the gravesites for a sort of spiritual stimulus or to ask for intercession (whether from God or from the rabbi deliberately remains vague): for a marriage partner, a child, occupational success, or spiritual enlightenment. Near some tombs bits of colored cloth hang on a sort of clothesline and flutter in the breeze, apparently a type of "I was here" graffiti; they reminded John and me of the Buddhist prayer flags we had seen in Mongolia.

The tomb of Rabbi Yehuda Hanasi, "Judah the Prince," was an elaborate stone structure, and the cool, dark room had dozens of niches in the walls for placing candles. Two well-dressed Yemenite Jewish men with *kippot* were standing outside next to their car. When they saw the seven of us together, with walking poles, backpacks, and map in hand, one asked, "What kind of group are you?"

John stepped up and smiled. "We're Messianic Jews hiking the Israel Trail."

They introduced themselves as Naphtali and Daniel and told us they had met Messianic Jews before. "Well done!" they said. "Did you know you are performing a good deed? God commanded us in Genesis, 'Go forth.'"

"We also read the Bible and I'd like to give you a paper we wrote about our trek," John offered. "And if you're ever in Eilat, come to our hostel."

Walking farther we came to a natural forest with an under-growth of bushes, flowers, and grass. A Bedouin woman in a long green sack-like dress with a scarf covering her hair was bent over gathering leaves out of the grass into a bag. Two small boys were laughing and playing nearby.

"*Kef Halek*! ("How are you?" in Arabic)," Karen called out as she and I approached the woman and tried to determine exactly what she was gathering. The woman pointed to the plant, showed us the large green leaf, and attempted in Arabic to explain its use.

I tried to imagine this woman's life—plucking leaves, perhaps some sort of native spinach, on the hills of Galilee. She seemed centuries removed from our bustling existence in town; she reminded me of the kind of woman Jesus could have encountered.

"Here, let me take a picture of you girls," John said, and the three of us lined up, our arms over each other's shoulders.

We eventually emerged from the forest into Mashad, an Arab town, and followed the Trail signs down the main street. We felt conspicuous with seven people.

As we paraded down the road, we noticed a couple of young women on a balcony. Since we had left the forest cover we felt the sun beating on our heads; we had shed our jackets.

"Would you happen to have some water for us?" John called up to the women, waving his empty water bottle. "We're on the Israel Trail."

A dark-haired teenager in jeans soon stepped out the front door, a water container in her hands. She spoke Hebrew.

"We're a group of Jews and non-Jews who believe that Isa, Jesus, is the Messiah," John told her.

"I also believe in Jesus," the girl said.

*Perhaps she's a Christian*, I thought, knowing that many Christian Arabs lived in Nazareth and its vicinity.

"He's one of our prophets together with Abraham, Moses, and David. They were all Muslims, and Mohammed is the final prophet," she added.

Of course I then understood that she was Muslim; I also knew we could not explain to her in a short time the difference between Jesus and Mohammed.

"Try reading the Injil (the New Testament) sometime," John

suggested. "Come to visit us in Eilat!"

"*Shukran*! (thank you). *Ma'asalameh*! (good-bye)." We waved our farewell.

Nearly adjacent to Mashad is the city of Nazareth Ilit, Upper Nazareth, a relatively new city with a large population of Russian immigrants. Below Nazareth Ilit is the older city of Nazareth, the largest Arab city in Israel and the capital of the North District. According to the New Testament, Nazareth was the hometown of Mary and Joseph. In Nazareth an angel appeared to Mary to announce she would "be with child and give Him the name Jesus." He would be called "the Son of the Most High and reign over the house of Jacob forever" (Lk. 1:31-33).

With its elaborate Basilica of the Annunciation and many other churches, Nazareth attracts Christian pilgrims from all over the world. One can even visit the "Synagogue Church," the traditional site of the synagogue which the young Jesus attended, and where he later read from the scroll of Isaiah. With nearly every event in the Bible linked to a location in Israel, "The Mount of Precipice," a hill on the edge of town, commemorates where the people from Nazareth became furious after hearing Jesus proclaim that "no prophet is accepted in his hometown." They "drove him out of town and took him to the brow of the hill on which the town was built, in order to throw him down the cliff," (Lk. 4:24, 29).

Arabs and Jews live next to each other here, their lives interwoven in so many ways. For the most part they dwell in peace one with another, although there is an underlying tension that makes a small incident capable of setting off an explosion. As we trekked through the land, viewing the daily lives of the two peoples up close, and experiencing their warmth and hospitality, we were convinced that the only way to peace in the Middle East is with God—only He is able to sort out the tangle.

We reached the car which we had parked in a supermarket parking lot in Nazareth Ilit in the morning. Our group posed for a final picture with Mt. Tabor in the background. Everyone agreed that it had been an incredible experience to walk for a day on the *Shvil*, and Hanan said he hoped to hike with us again. On their way back to Haifa, they dropped us off at Tal and Adi's, the cheese makers, who had invited us to spend the night.

Mt. Tabor's rounded hump rising above the surrounding valleys is visible for miles in every direction. The early Christians designated it as the Mount of Transfiguration, commemorating the occasion when Jesus went up to "a high mountain" with three of His disciples. Moses and Elijah appeared before them while Jesus' face "shone like the sun, and His clothes became as white as the light," (Mt. 17:1, 2).

Early in our trek we had come to the conclusion that the Trail planners had attempted to include as many mountains as possible in the Trail's route. It seemed that if there was a mountain anywhere in our vicinity, we were certain to climb it. Thus we weren't surprised that the *Shvil* led us up and over Mt. Tabor. At 567 meters above sea level, it isn't massive or lofty, but its uniform, conical shape and its isolation make it striking. It looks like a child's crayon drawing of a mountain. No wonder it's been a holy site since ancient times.

Two imposing churches stand on the summit. We were told at the restaurant at the base of the mountain that it was a forty-five minute climb, but because we stopped and talked to people on the way, it took us an hour to reach the top. A class of religious girls from Ofra, a town in the West Bank, was unusually friendly and polite to us, and even our poles didn't elicit the usual joke.

"What about your sticks?" one of the teachers, a man of about our age, asked. "Do they really help you?"

"Sure," John responded. "At our age you need them for your knees. We're Messianic Jews on the Israel Trail."

"Do you know Moshav Yad Hashmona?" he asked. "They're like you."

"Sure, they're our friends," I told them. "We slept there a few weeks ago, on our way north."

I was continually surprised at how respectful the religious Jews were of our faith. In Eilat we rarely met these people. Our trekking the land seemed to soften their hearts toward us.

Mt. Tabor is a highlight on many Christian Holy Land tours, but we met an equal number of Israelis on the mountain. Mt. Tabor is mentioned a number of times in the Old Testament. In the book of Judges, for example, we read about Deborah the prophetess and Barak, her general, routing the Canaanite army under Sisera's command on Mt. Tabor.

The last section of the trail, before the summit, was steep and having lost the markers for a short time, we found ourselves bushwhacking through dense brush. When we eventually emerged out of the thicket, three tourists with binoculars were admiring the stunning view. They turned their gaze to stare at the two people with large packs and hiking sticks who appeared in front of them.

"Are you John Pex?" the young man asked.

We were startled; but Israel is a small country. John looked at him, trying to remember.

"How did you know?"

"I'm a volunteer at Yad Hashmona and I stayed in your hostel a few months ago," he said. "But I'm sure you can't remember everyone who comes to you."

We spoke for a few minutes and explained to them about our journey on the Israel Trail before continuing on the path.

The trail made nearly a complete circle around the peak. John and I were gaining a new excitement for Israel's geography. I remembered how I had dreaded climbing mountains in the beginning of our journey. Now I enjoyed being able to look back from where we had come and to gaze ahead to where the Trail was taking us. The Carmel Ridge was visible to the west and the Golan Heights rose above the Sea of Galilee to the east. Northward were the hills and ridges of the lower Galilee with Mt. Meron rising above the rest. The multi-colored fields of the Jezreel Valley stretched out in a colorful patchwork pattern.

I tried not to think about going home in three days or about whether we would return to the Trail afterwards.

*Never mind,* I told myself. *God has led us so far, and He'll make it clear to us both what we should do. He knows I'd love to finish.*

An hour's walk brought us down the far side of Mt. Tabor. We were looking forward to reaching the Sea of Galilee the next day.

While eating dinner that night in a restaurant at the base of the mountain, we struck up a conversation with the waitress, Sivan. When we told her we managed The Shelter Hostel in Eilat, she asked if she could bring a group to our hostel, the "Victims of Terror Attacks." Sivan introduced us to her friend Mohammed, and explained that they had both been wounded in a terror attack two years previously. They became friends in the hospital and found they could understand one another in a manner that other people weren't able to. Mohammed still couldn't work and often came to visit her at the restaurant. Sivan was interested in reading the New Testament, so we promised to send her one when we reached home.

We started out walking the next day with high expectations.

"Who ever walks from Eilat to the Sea of Galilee?" John said.

Most of the Galilee, the northern region of Israel, is sparsely populated. I could see on the map that we wouldn't cross a road all day, nor would we be going near any settlements. This region consists mostly of rocky, mountainous terrain, thus the towns, villages and roads are relatively few. The ample rainfall and comparatively low temperatures of the Galilee provide a hospitable environment for wildlife and plant life.

Mt. Tabor remained a towering presence behind us for hours as we hiked beside yellow mustard plants and shining green wheat fields. Two small lakes created by a dam were nestled between the green hills.

"Looks like Switzerland," John remarked.

"Because it's green? Maybe like Scotland, too. That's green, but without the high peaks. Anyway, it's pretty different from the scenery we're used to in the south."

We heard a kind of barking or cackling in the air above us and strained our eyes as we looked up to search the heavens. Squinting, we saw hundreds of black spots high in the sky, moving towards us. They seemed to be jabbering to each other, and we could see the typical black and white markings of storks. Circling and gliding gracefully on thermals, they steadily proceeded northwards, on their way from their African winter grounds to their summer home in Europe. Flock after large flock continued passing over us and the storks' chattering followed us for hours.

Twice a year, birds soar over Israel, the land bridge between Asia and Europe and Africa, on an unsurpassed scale. Studies have shown that 500 million birds cross Israel in the course of their migrations. I've developed the habit of glancing up to see if there are any storks, eagles, hawks, or other birds overhead whenever I step outside during the spring and fall.

Farther on we came to a flowing stream. I sat down to remove my shoes; John was already jumping from rock to rock. I was thankful for the opportunity to rest and remove my boots. The cool water lapping around my feet made them tingle. John, as usual, enjoyed the challenge of the crossing, whether over stones or a fallen log.

On the other side of the *wadi* a class of high school children was sitting and eating sandwiches. Their teacher, a woman our age, spoke to us and asked about our route. When we said we were on the Israel Trail, she told us that she had hiked it three years earlier. She turned to the class and announced, "This couple is hiking the *Shvil Israel*."

The whole class began to clap. We stood there and looked at each other, not accustomed to being applauded just because we were hiking through the land of Israel. I didn't feel like a hero or star; after all, we were just doing something that we loved.

Rising out of one valley, the jeep road we followed passed through fields before descending into another valley that would lead us down to the Sea of Galilee. In the distance a strange sight appeared. Two men were walking through the middle of the alfalfa field towards us. One was holding a map, and they appeared to be carrying small backpacks. By their dress—black *kippas* on their heads and the white garment with fringes that is normally worn under the shirt but which they had on over their clothes—we could tell they were religious. We assumed they were older men and were lost. Maybe we could help them. As they drew closer, however, we saw they were quite young, not older than seventeen or eighteen, and that they were simply taking a short-cut through the cropland.

"Shalom!" they greeted us. "Are you on the I.T.?"

John looked a bit bewildered, but I quickly realized they meant the Israel Trail. We had just learned the "in" way to refer to it. So I answered affirmatively.

The young men, Israel and Jacob, told us they had set out six days ago from Kibbutz Dan to hike the entire trail. They were glad to meet us; we were the first fellow *Shvil* hikers they'd met.

"Let's take a photo," Jacob said enthusiastically.

"I'll hold your poles," Israel said, smiling for the camera.

"Where's all your gear?" John asked.

Israel explained that they had started out with full packs but found them too heavy, so they left their tent and sleeping pads behind. It had unfortunately rained heavily the previous night, and they had spent half the morning drying themselves and their gear in the sun. Later that night, when it rained again, we thought of them, and doubted that they would succeed in completing the *Shvil*.

At the highest point on our path, we relaxed in the shade of an aged, spreading oak, and contemplated the breathtaking view. A flock of storks in V-formation was flying below us. Green fields were spread out beneath them, extending to the blue waters of the Sea of Galilee.

Being on a mountaintop reminded me that in Hebrew, a prophet was sometimes called a *ro-ee*, translated into English as seer. *Ro-ee* is taken from the Hebrew word "to see." When we are up high, we can see far into the distance in all directions, which a prophet does in the spiritual sense. Being on a peak is exhilarating but also a little scary, because I can see how far we still have to travel. The prophets must have felt overwhelmed when they received a message directly from God. But how frightening for them when they were given harsh messages concerning Israel's future. Isaiah was told that the king of Assyria, Israel's enemy and a mighty world power, would "sweep on into Judah" (Isa. 8: 8). Jeremiah prophesied that all nations will serve Nebuchadnezzar, king of Babylon (Jer. 27:6,7).

Not knowing anything about the future or what to expect can also be unnerving. Earlier in the day when we trekked through a *wadi* with nearly impenetrable bushes, I couldn't even distinguish John in front of me. Most of the time we hiked through territory that was somewhere in between the mountaintop and the *wadi*. That's life, too.

In Hebrew the Sea of Galilee is called *Kinneret*, which has the same root letters as harp, the musical instrument that King David used to praise God. The harp-shaped Sea of Galilee seems to nestle in the hollow created by the Great Rift Valley. The waters were perfectly calm that day, as they usually are. But we knew that a storm could arise quickly on the sea, stirring up the water into high waves, as happened to Jesus and His disciples when they were crossing in a boat. (Lk. 8:22, 23.) While camping with our children on the Sea of Galilee we had experienced severe storms several times.

A filmy haze hung over the lake, nearly obscuring the Golan Heights that rose sharply above the opposite shore. The Jordan River's exit from the lake was barely discernible. As the twisting river flowed southward towards the Dead Sea, it was only visible as a line of dense dark-green foliage.

We began our long descent towards the sea. Part way down the slope an old car was parked under an oak tree; not far from it an elderly gentleman was scouring the hillside for plants and popping them into his bag. He walked over to us and introduced himself to us as Mufti from Shibli. The village's residents are members of a Bedouin tribe which has settled permanently at the foot of Mount Tabor. We knew that they have adapted their lifestyle to the 21st century, leaving behind many of the ancient customs, but it was refreshing to observe Mufti gathering traditional food. He spoke excellent Hebrew and gladly accepted one of our pamphlets.

"My son lives in America," Mufti told us, "but I have no desire to go abroad. I'm seventy years old, and I'm happy here."

He showed us the contents of his sack. "They're like wild artichokes. You boil them for half an hour with onions and olive oil and it's healthy—better than meat."

We didn't doubt the health benefits of Mufti's lifestyle, but couldn't help wondering whether his grandchildren would be found out here in the future gathering wild artichokes, as they were changing from the lifestyle of herders and gatherers to modern village and city dwellers.

We emerged from the *wadi* with its dense underbrush. The land leveled out and soon we were walking through a banana plantation. Several of the green bunches of bananas had a yellowish tinge.

"I'd love to eat a self-plucked banana!" I said. To trek through the land and eat its produce held an allure for me.

"Not me," responded John. "They're not ripe."

I quickly discovered that John was right—they were impossible to peel.

We plunged into thick reeds and emerged on the banks of the Jordan River. The towering eucalyptus trees typical of this area, provided shade for our jeep trail. Eucalyptus trees played a significant role in making modern Israel habitable. Many of the early settlers died of malaria. By the 1890s eucalyptus trees were planted; their roots, as effective as any hydraulic pump, lowered the water table and drained the swamps where the malaria-carrying mosquitoes bred.

Five young Israelis were lying on blankets in a clearing, a pot of tea bubbling on a campfire next to them. Just as we approached, one of the men dove into the water and took a few quick strokes.

"Cold water?" John called out to him.

He swam to the other side and shook the water out of his long wavy black hair. "It's okay," he called back.

Except for Mufti and the two religious boys without the tent, we hadn't met anyone all day, so John was in the mood to talk. "Where you guys from?"

"From Tiberias," Izzy, a tall young man who was the spokesman of the group, replied. "This is where we come to take it easy."

"We're on the Israel Trail, thirty-six days since Eilat. Here's a paper we wrote about our journey," John said.

"Cool," Izzy responded.

John obviously felt a kinship with these young people, maybe because swimming and making tea on a fire are two of his favorite activities. "We swim in the Red Sea; it was there, years ago, that we started to believe that *Yeshua* is the Messiah."

"How can you be sure that He's the one, especially since our rabbis didn't accept Him?"

"*Yeshua* wandered around this very area, and thousands of Jewish people did believe in Him. It was the religious leaders of His day, just like many religious leaders today, who were afraid of His influence. Even in Israel today, thousands of Jews believe in *Yeshua*. My wife is Jewish," John said turning to me.

John was warming up to the discussion and looked as if he could go on for hours. I was feeling more tired by the minute as well as extremely thirsty. We still had to reach the Sea of Galilee, and the sun was getting low in the sky. I signaled to John with my eyes.

I felt bad to hurry my husband away from a chance to talk about our faith, but John tends to lose track of time in these situations, and he hadn't looked at the map recently.

"Sorry, I guess we'd better be going," John excused himself. "Come to Eilat and we'll talk more."

It was nearly dark by the time we reached the lake, but John couldn't be stopped. We walked straight to the closest beach where he stripped off his dirty shirt and pants and dove in.

"We walked to the Kinneret! Can you believe it?" John shouted happily back to me from the chilly waters.

I discovered that finding a place to stay when you're on foot is different than if you have a car. After walking all day, we didn't have the energy to veer far off the Trail. We didn't have any good friends nearby and I wasn't in the mood to visit with someone I didn't really know. Thankfully we were directed to a guest house on the lake, up the road one kilometer, my limit that evening.

In bed that night I pictured us going home the next day. We planned to walk till early afternoon before our friend, Steve, would meet us and drive us to the Tiberias bus station. Tomorrow we would sleep in our own bed. But would we succeed in returning to finish the Trail?

# 14. A Pause, or the End?

We awoke to the music of pattering rain and prepared for a new Trail experience: walking in mud. It was a small miracle that we had hiked thirty-six days without getting rained out even once.

By the time we had finished breakfast and began hiking, the sky was still gray but the shower had ceased. Nevertheless, the dark earth around Tiberias had turned into a thick, sticky sludge which stuck to our boots as we slogged along, adding at least an extra kilogram of weight to each foot. I felt as if I were walking on broad platform shoes. We had to stop frequently to scrape the heavy, gooey pads of mud off onto rocks.

The trail led us through the historic settlement of Kinneret whose history began towards the end of the nineteenth century. At that time a movement of young Jewish men and women from Europe began to take seriously what the Bible said about the land of Israel. One such Scripture was Leviticus 25:23: "The land must not be sold permanently, for the land is Mine."

Their goal became redemption of the land, including both purchase and reclamation.

Through complicated bureaucratic procedures, rich benefactors succeeded in buying property from the local Turkish officials, representatives of the governing Ottoman Empire. Reclamation involved reversing the effects of centuries of environmental neglect by draining swamps, rebuilding terraces and stone walls, and creating functioning settlements, all attempted by enthusiastic visionaries with absolutely no experience in agriculture.

Today in Kinneret, pleasant homes with spacious flower gardens are interspersed with older looking, black stone buildings—a tribute to the pioneers whose idealism led them to this forsaken corner of the world one hundred years ago. In the nearby cemetery, the gravestones testify to the heavy toll their strenuous lives exacted.

A couple who were hiking with small backpacks approached us on the path above Tiberias. As they drew closer we were surprised to see they were about our age. We were used to seeing younger people on the trails.

"Are you on the *Shvil*?" the husband asked. He went on to explain that they were also walking the Israel Trail, but were taking it one day a week. Living in Haifa, he explained, the logistics were a bit complicated, and they didn't know how they would continue when they reached the sections of the Trail farther from home. They had been driving out to each week's beginning point in the morning, then taking a bus back to their car at the end of the day. But they were having to start earlier and earlier every time, and the bus connections weren't always easy.

"And what do you do for showers?" inquired the wife.

"Do we smell so much?" I later said to John, laughing.

They seemed pleased to meet us and wished us well. We continued towards Tiberias.

Tiberias is built on the side of a hill and is divided into upper and lower sections. After walking through the streets of Upper Tiberias, we headed for the Horns of Hittim, a noticeable landmark with its twin humps. Unfortunately, soon after leaving the town, we completely lost the path. One minute we were walking along a plainly-marked jeep road, and then suddenly we realized we hadn't seen the trail logo for some time.

People often asked us if we ever lost the Trail signs, and we replied, "Every day." Sometimes the symbol was covered by vegetation; other times construction projects obscured the signs. Or else, as in this case, we were striding happily along a road when abruptly, without warning, the trail veered off. We simply hadn't been paying attention. It reminded me of how we can be carrying on complacently in life along a broad path with many footsteps and not notice a narrow path diverging off it. Even when the trail looks obvious, or perhaps especially during those times, it is essential that we continue to look for God's trail markers.

The signs eluded us for an hour, at the end of which time I found myself bushwhacking through a field of wheat up to my midriff.

"Just follow in my footsteps," John called back to me. "I'm forging a path through here."

But it wasn't so simple. The wheat stalks closed behind him, and I felt as if I were shuffling through water—each step was an effort. I remembered reading that walking in water was an especially effective exercise for the calves and thighs. I could believe that! Like sailors focusing on a distant beacon, we fixed our gaze on a lone oak tree on the summit of Mount Arbel to guide us to our destination.

The Horns of Hittim are famous for several reasons. The prophet Jethro, Moses' father-in-law, is buried at the Horns of Hittim. They are also the site where on July 4, 1187, Saladin, the Kurdish ruler of Egypt, faced the combined forces of the kings of the Crusader Kingdom of Jerusalem and of Tripoli. The debilitated and thirst-crazed Crusader army, weighed down by their heavy armor, was decimated in what became a major disaster for the Crusaders and a turning point in the history of the Crusades.

The Horns of Hittim are named Nebi Shue'ib, after the chief Druze prophet. His tomb is an important pilgrimage site. The

Druze religious sect developed out of Islam in the tenth century.
Today over two million Druze reside in the mountainous areas
of Lebanon, Syria, Jordan, and Israel. Publicly they are closed
concerning the details of their faith, concealing their true beliefs
and tenets. Only to the minority of their members who choose to
become religious and follow a pious lifestyle are the mysteries of
their doctrines revealed. The "ignorant ones," as the outer group
are called, accept the faith on the basis of tradition and culture.

The Druze believe that everyone alive today is a reincarnation
of someone who lived during the generation after the initial revelation of their religion, at which time everyone was invited to join.
Thus anyone who was meant to be Druze is one already. As a
result, they don't accept converts and they discourage their followers from converting to other religions. A Druze who intermarries
or converts is totally ostracized from his people. Their community
identification is exceptionally strong. At the same time, as a minority wherever they live, the Druze endeavor to blend in among
the nation in which they live in order to protect themselves from
persecution. In Israel this attitude has led them to be exemplary
citizens and soldiers.

Our friend Steve was waiting for us on the rocky crest of
Mount Arbel. He lives on a *moshav* in the area. For 5½ hours we
hadn't sat down or eaten—not even a granola bar. Such an effort
would have been unthinkable in the beginning of our journey.

"Shall we have some lunch?" asked Steve. "Or wait for the
sandwiches and tea I have in my car?"

"I'm not even hungry," I replied.

Following Steve down the Arbel Cliff, the side of the Horns
facing the Sea of Galilee, was simple. With Steve in the lead,
I didn't even have to consult our map. The steep path had iron
handholds drilled into some of the nearly-vertical sections, and it
passed many caves in the cliff on the way. Some of the caves were
like multi-storied mansions, incorporating an elaborate system of

rooms and passageways. They were already in use in 40 B.C., when rebel Galilean Jews took a stand against Herod the Great.

After coming off the sharp descent, we followed Steve through avocado and loquat groves to Migdal, a small town north of Tiberias, where his car was parked. Migdal was the home of Mary Magdalene, whose name in Hebrew is "Miriam from Migdal."

Steve drove us to the Tiberias bus station, and a few minutes later a minibus was taking us to Tel Aviv. We stared out the window throughout the two-and-a-half hour trip—like watching a video on fast forward. Whizzing by, we covered ground that had taken us two weeks on foot. We were excited to recognize familiar sites.

We passed by Mt. Tabor and the backside of Mt. Carmel. Had we really climbed those mountains? We drove by Caesarea, and the Purple Iris Reserve. Crossing Nahal Hadera we caught a glimpse of "our" sign on the bridge railing. Finally, arriving at the small airport in north Tel Aviv, we spotted an Israel Trail sign on a lamppost.

Waiting for the plane, I had time to think, and a mixture of emotions welled inside me. Of course I was happy to go home—thankful for a home to return to—but I would rather have completed the trip before returning to Eilat. Rain was predicted in the Galilee for the next few days, and we would likely have been holed up somewhere along the trail if we had stayed, waiting for the storm to pass. I had no doubt we were doing the right thing, sending Jim off properly. He had given us an amazing gift of his time, enabling us to "walk the land." I still was troubled, though, by the uncertainty of whether we would finish our trek.

"If not this year, then next," John said cheerfully.

Everything depended on the situation at home and whether they could manage without us. We had reserved a return flight to Tel Aviv for Sunday morning, the day after Jim's party, but weren't sure we would use it.

At the same time, I was looking further ahead. I wondered how I would feel when we actually finished—a sense of satisfaction? But perhaps also emptiness? I had plenty to keep me occupied at home, and I enjoyed my life and routine. Was that all? What next? Sitting in the terminal I wrote in my diary:

- *I can't let those at home feel I don't want to be there.*
- *Though plans sometimes don't work out as we hoped, it's not a disappointment.*
- *We had a dream and fulfilled it.*
- *We couldn't have done it without total passion and commitment.*
- *I pray God will use this experience even long afterwards, through my pictures, or the book I plan to write, or in other ways we can't begin to imagine.*

As the bright lights of Eilat came into view and the small plane bumped onto the runway, my heart beat wildly and my stomach churned. Was this a pause, or the end of our walk?

The next morning, one of the first things John did was to cancel our flight back to Tel Aviv.

"I just can't be sure," he said. "There's too much going on here and they need me. ... Maybe later in the week."

For someone like me who tries to complete every project I start and do things in an orderly manner, this was a test of faith. But I trusted John's judgment. We had prayed about our journey before we had begun two months previously, and had experienced God's guidance every step of the way. My bad knee could have stopped us before we started, or cold and stormy weather, or any number of other circumstances. So if we were meant to continue, I knew the door would open.

We combined a farewell party for Jim with a celebration of John's fifty-ninth birthday. We had many stories to tell our friends and our two youngest children: Moriah, who was managing the Shelter, and Yonatan, who was on leave for the weekend from the navy. I began checking my e-mails and sorting our pictures on the computer. But even as I went through the motions, my thoughts were on the flowering, verdant *wadi*s of the Galilee.

By Sunday, Moriah insisted she could handle the hostel another week, and the staff encouraged us to leave. So we felt peace to return to the Trail early Tuesday morning. I wasn't nervous when we took off this time—I knew what to expect and what to bring. Hiking the Israel Trail had become how we spent our time; it was our life.

# 15. The Final Stretch

Immersed again in the pungent smell of mustard flowers and surrounded by humid greenness and animated bird songs, I glided along the trail as if in a dream.

By catching an early flight to Tel Aviv on Tuesday, a bus to Tiberias, and a taxi to the trailhead, we were already back on the *Shvil* at 10:45 A.M., at the same spot where we had left off in Migdal.

Soon we were out of the avocado, orange, and olive groves and entering Nahal Amud ("the pillar stream") named for the huge natural rock column near the beginning of the *wadi*. There we met an older couple from Jerusalem who were out for a short hike. They asked if we were retired.

"Not quite," John replied.

Later we passed a group of seventh graders from a religious boys' school. The children were well-mannered and friendly, and as usual asked about our poles.

"We're on our way to Mt. Hermon," John explained.

"So where are your skis then?" one smart boy inquired.

"They'll rent them," their teacher answered.

The vegetation was lush, colorful, and dense. The trail had us criss-crossing the narrow gurgling stream, jumping from rock to rock, and passing through tunnels carved out of the reeds.

We met three young men with large backpacks, and instantly identified them as Israel Trail hikers. They told us they had begun five days ago. They were curious about us.

"How old are you?" the one named Udi asked.

When we told them our ages, another one, Boaz, said, "Way to go!"

I hoped we were a good example to these young hikers.

I remembered in my nomadic hippy life that I had occasionally met older travelers who smoked drugs and listened to our music. Today I shudder when I remember those people who were trapped in a lifestyle that became a prolonged escape from responsibility. They were Peter Pan types who seemed to say, "I don't want to grow up!" Yet young people are always searching for role models, and those older hippies had been an inspiration to me; I had been encouraged to find that life didn't stop at thirty. Now with Jesus in my life I have so much more reason to live and to share.

"Come to the Shelter when you finish and your first night is free," John told the young men.

We exchanged information about the different *Shvil* segments. They asked about obtaining water in the south. I was concerned about our following day's climb up Mt. Meron, the highest mountain on the Trail, but they assured me it wasn't really that difficult.

We weren't rushing; we planned to meet Steve at a road just ten kilometers from our starting point. We even had time to stretch out in the grass and flowers next to the path, where John instantly fell asleep and took a short nap.

Our timing was perfect; we met Steve and his wife, Rose, as they were returning home from the grocery store. We were close to their *moshav* where Steve worked as a shepherd.

The first time we had met Steve—through mutual friends—was when he drove three hours to Arad to hike with us in the Small Crater and drive our packs to the campground at the end of that trail segment. The second time, he met us on top of the Arbel Cliff and after the long descent, drove us to the Tiberias bus station. Finally we had the pleasure of visiting Steve in his home and meeting Rose, who had sent the delicious meal of chicken, beans, potatoes, and cookies to us when we were carrying all our food on our backs.

As a hiker himself, Steve understood our eagerness to start early the next morning. So we set out in the wonder of dawn, enjoying the fresh, cool air, and the muted colors.

We walked on a wide jeep path. We were disappointed that here Nahal Amud was dry. But soon we passed a sign that read, *For good hikers only.* The path narrowed and water appeared in the streambed. The sound of the brook cascading over the rocks mixed with birdsongs to provide perfect background music. As we worked our way through the long narrow canyon, the trail began climbing the rocks high above the stream. This was just the kind of path I liked—interesting but not dangerous, with striking views on all sides.

After many ascents, descents, and rock scrambles, the trail forded the rushing stream, the first of multiple crossings. My poles kept me from tumbling into the rushing water.

We heard the rumble of Amud Falls before we saw them—the *wadi* plunged ten meters over a cliff to form a natural pool with a gravel beach. On a warmer day we would have enjoyed a swim and a shoulder massage under the waterfall. In the summer, however, the falls would likely be reduced to a trickle.

In the woods of Nahal Amud we found a bizarre phenomenon. At random spots along the path, the wildflowers and other plants were uprooted, leaving bare ground. Someone with shovels, hoes, or even heavier equipment appeared to have dug up large stretches of ground underneath the sizable oriental plane, oak, and carob trees.

"It's so ugly!" I said, not comprehending why anyone would destroy bushes and ground cover in a nature reserve.

When we saw the scene repeated, John said, "There must be an explanation. Maybe someone was murdered around here and the police are looking for the body. Looks like a whole team's been excavating with shovels and pickaxes."

Another mystery to us was the many ruins in this *wadi*—substantial stone buildings and arched bridges. Why in the isolated Nahal Amud, of all places?

Both puzzles were solved when we met a Druze ranger from the Nature Protection Society, at the Sechvi Pools. Although it was only 10:30, I was hungry, so we decided to stop for an early lunch in this idyllic picnic spot.

We sat on the natural stone steps leading down to the shallow pools, which in fact is one pool divided by rows of rocks, giving the impression of many separate basins.

"Who did all this building in such an out-of-the-way *wadi*?" John asked the ranger, who said his name was Karam.

He told us that, when the Jews were expelled from Spain and Portugal in 1492, many arrived in Thessaloniki Greece where they learned the wool trade. When they migrated from there to Safed, an historic city on the hill above Nahal Amud, they brought their expertise with them. Safed became a center for the production of high-quality woolen fabrics exported to customers all over Europe. Textile merchants built mechanical "fulling" mills that used the waters of Nahal Amud to turn the wool into felt. A flourishing industry developed. After the Ottomans exiled a thousand Safed families to Cyprus in the sixteenth century, most of the town's textile industry was destroyed and the fulling mills were converted into flour mills. These, along with the ancient bridges, were the relics we had seen.

I wanted to know who had been making such a mess of the woods. So I asked Karam, "Why is all the ground torn up?"

"Wild boars," he replied. "There are plenty of them around here. Be careful if you run into one—they can be aggressive." I remembered hearing that boars have nasty tempers, but I couldn't remember if they attacked people. Afterwards I realized I should have asked Karam more about the boars' behavior, and what to do if we were confronted by one.

Around the pools, carpets of green grass and multi-colored flowers grew under the huge Atlantic pistachio and plane trees. Fig trees filled the air with their sweet, fruity scent. Sechvi was evidently a popular spot for groups. We saw Russian religious girls, Arab children, and young boys with long side locks intermingling amidst the water and vegetation.

Two trim, rugged-looking older men with white hair and short beards, small backpacks, and hiking boots were resting on the rocks. Though they definitely weren't the typical after-the-army *Shvil* hikers, we had developed a radar for folks who were on the Israel Trail. It was time for an early lunch, so we settled on a boulder next to them and found our hunch was correct: Ben and Israel, though ten years older than we, were also on the Trail. They planned to hike the northern half this season, as far as Jerusalem. Having begun their journey with heavy packs, camping out every night, they were finding the undertaking much more achievable since two days ago when they left most of their gear with friends in Safed.

"What made you decide to hike the Trail?" Ben asked.

"For us it's a spiritual journey," John answered. "A chance to get close to God in nature and to connect with this land. We're Messianic Jews, believing in the Old and the New Testaments and that *Yeshua*, Jesus, is our Messiah."

"I'm an atheist," Israel told John, "but I don't mind talking about different faiths."

In this respect, he was typical of many people we meet—open for a discussion of various philosophies but unwilling to commit himself. John and I were the same until, through personally reading the Bible, we came to the conclusion that Jesus, the Messiah of

Israel and of the whole world, is the only truth. John loves this sort of dialogue, and has much patience for reasoning and explaining; we were all enjoying our pause in the shade next to the water. But finally we stood up and excused ourselves, and left the pools.

We met many school classes; in some places the path was as busy as a boardwalk. As we wove our way through a group of teenage religious girls hiking in long skirts over pants, their teacher stopped us.

"Where are you from?" she asked, guiding us to a position facing the students.

We found ourselves being interviewed. The girls flung out questions. "How long ... far ... heavy ...?"

The teacher smiled patiently, obviously pleased to have discovered an educational opportunity.

As we finally took our leave and waved good-bye, I overheard one girl say to her friend, "When I'm married I'd like to do the *Shvil Israel* with my husband."

Many of the school children wore matching T-shirts, though in passing I couldn't read the Hebrew inscription quickly enough to understand who or what they represented. Moreover, some who wore the T-shirts were speaking Hebrew and others Arabic; some were secular and others religious; so they clearly weren't from the same school.

John found a friendly-looking teacher and introduced himself. "What sort of group are you, with your shirts?"

"My name is Hamud," the teacher said, smiling. "Today is the national clean-up day on the trails," he explained. "Druze, Arab, and Jewish—we're all out cleaning the national parks. I teach in a Druze school."

John pulled a tract out of his pocket, gave it to the teacher, and invited him to The Shelter. "Come to Eilat sometime!"

We came to a picnic area next to a road. Two young men were lying on the ground under a tree, their shoes off. Apparently the season for hiking the Israel Trail was beginning. Every day we were meeting fellow hikers. We had evidently started earlier than most. We were like a pair of migrating storks who finally discover the rest of their flock.

The young men, Ben and Niv, told us they'd started out enthusiastically three days before in Kibbutz Dan, walking thirty-two kilometers the first day. The next day their feet were so blistered they could barely limp. Now, they told us, they'd learned to walk in moderation.

"When you finish the Trail," John told them, "your first night in the Shelter is free."

They never took up our offer; the following summer we found out why, when in August, on the hottest day of the year at 45°C, Ben arrived in the Shelter.

"We only reached as far as the Kinneret," he told us. "By that time my feet were one big bloody mess. But I'm starting again tomorrow from Taba."

"What?!" John cried. "In this heat? And alone? Don't even think about it! How much water did you plan to carry?"

"I'll take six one-and-a-half liter bottles. If I don't do it now, I'll never have the time. I'm starting college in the fall."

"Okay. I'll leave you another six bottles by the Israel Trail sign on the road," said John. "And take my cell phone number, in case you need me."

Ben left the hostel at 7 A.M. At 4 P.M. John's phone rang.

"I'm out of water," Ben stuttered weakly. "Can you come?" He described his position. He was only a kilometer from where John had stashed the water bottles.

"I can't walk another step; I'm dehydrated," said Ben.

We jumped in the car, drove fifteen minutes to where the *Shvil* intersected the road, placed four bottles in our pack, and hurried down the path. Twenty minutes later we found Ben collapsed in the shade under an overhanging rock.

"My water was finished at 1:30 already," he said. "I rested for a while, but had no choice but to keep going. There was no phone reception in the narrow canyon. My lips are parched, but I'm thankful I didn't start hallucinating."

I've never seen anyone enjoy water so much. By the time we came back to the car, all four bottles were empty.

"It's not every day you get to save someone's life," I said.

Of course when we met Ben at the base of Mt. Meron, this adventure was far in the future.

"Took us six hours to reach here from the other side of the mountain," Niv said.

From the map I knew we had far to go. Now I felt an urgency.

"It's past noon. We'd better get going," I pressed. Our route led us directly over the top of the twelve-hundred-meter peak, the highest in Israel prior to the Six-Day War, when Mt. Hermon came into Israel's hands.

Some Christian scholars consider Mt. Meron an alternate site for the Mount of Transfiguration. Those who support this view over Mt. Tabor, the traditional location, find evidence in geographical and chronological clues in the Scriptures.

An interesting Jewish tradition (the Jewish religion abounds with legends and superstitions) is an enormous upright rock column on the mountain known as "Elijah's Throne" or "The Throne of the Messiah." Jewish sages believe that here in the end of days Elijah will appear, sit on the stone, and blow his trumpet to herald the coming of the Messiah. Could this Jewish fable reflect a tradition that originated when Elijah joined Jesus the Messiah on the mountain where He was transfigured?

Mt. Meron is a magnet for religious Jews; many revered rabbis are buried there. Thankfully we weren't passing through a few months later. On the holiday of Lag B'Omer in May, the village of Meron on the mountain slope is transformed from a quiet, rural community to a boisterous pilgrimage site. Over 150,000 devotees from around the country gather to celebrate the anniversary of the death of the renowned Rabbi Shimon Bar Yochai. Although ostensibly they journey to partake of the rabbi's spiritual light, for many it is nothing more than a huge party, including barbeques, music, bonfires, and vendors hawking merchandise.

We trekked the upper slopes of Mt. Meron through lanes created by the rocks piled by Druze farmers to create terraces. One unusual wall was built, not with the customary field stones, but with old refrigerators piled on top of each other.

We were nearing the summit when our trail signs disappeared. A logo on a rock pointed down through a field into a cluster of trees, but the next marker was nowhere to be found. John and I separated and tried to systematically cover the hill, hoping to find our trail; but to no avail. We were losing precious time and it was getting late. An army outpost was visible on the summit. We knew the Trail passed by there.

"No problem," said John. "We'll just bushwhack in that direction." He relished opportunities to leave the beaten path.

Up and down the hillside we trudged, tacking back and forth through tangled thorn bushes, hauling ourselves over rocks. At one point I was leading the way on my hands and knees under a thick bramble, my hat off so I wouldn't lose it, and my hair constantly getting snagged by the spikes, when I heard distant voices.

"Thank God!" I said. "We must be close to the road."

I emerged from the undergrowth next to what looked and smelled like a small sewage treatment plant. The road was on the far side of a spread of what appeared to be dried mud. I charged across—and sunk into raw sewage over my boots. The foul slime splashed up both pant legs.

"Yuck!" I yelled. "Bring me the water! Pour it on my pants and boots!"

John emptied what was left in his water bottle, but it wasn't enough; the stench and blotches of sewage remained.

"Another bottle!"

John didn't hesitate as he poured the second bottle over me, our last, down to the last drop. I felt nearly clean, but now we had no water to drink. Never mind, it was late, the sun was low, we were heading downhill, and I hoped we wouldn't be thirsty.

Stepping out onto the road, we came upon the class of religious girls we'd met a few hours earlier in Nahal Amud. They were amazed to see us; they had driven up the mountain in a bus.

The path down Mt. Meron wandered through the forest with occasional views of the mountains in Lebanon. We met three more Israel Trail hikers and an American Jewish group.

The group's Israeli leader looked at us and said, "Hey! You're on the *Shvil*, right? I remember meeting you two weeks ago near Modi'in."

One of the women, when she heard about our walk, enthusiastically explained that they were on a tour emphasizing the link between Judaism and ecology.

"Eco-Jews," John said to me as they headed up the mountain. We had met groups like this before that blend Judaism with environmental issues, or the arts, or politics or other contemporary subjects attempting to make their religion more relevant today.

Reaching the road junction at 5:30 P.M. after eleven hours on the trail, one of our longest days, we hitchhiked to friends in an isolated settlement a few kilometers from the Lebanese border.


Our host, Yochanan, gave us an early start the next morning when he dropped us off at the trail on his way to work. We didn't expect to have a longer day than the previous one, our record till now. The freshness of the early morning was delightful. The dew, sprinkled on the grass and flowers, created a field of sparkling diamonds, and the steady hum of the crickets' chirping was as an orchestra accompanying us on our dance along the path.

Entering Nahal Tzivon we had one of those surprises that made walking the Trail such a treat. We immediately named it "the enchanted woods." For over an hour we hiked through a dense, dark forest in which the sun barely filtered through the leaves, forming random splotches of light. Obviously this was a rarely traveled segment of the trail. We felt almost as alone as in the desert. My heart beat rapidly as I rounded each twist in the path, like a wide-eyed child visiting an amusement park. Spongy moss and feathery ferns blanketed the rock walls and covered the boulders strewn on the way. Trees bent into exotic contortions, their roots exposed, forming natural steps. I felt as if we had entered Middle Earth of *Lord of the Rings*; I expected dwarfs or hobbits to pop from behind the bushes.

The book, *Israel Trail,* describes Nahal Tzivon as "one of the most beautiful sections of the *Shvil Israel*," and gives this section the maximum three stars. For once, I agreed.

As suddenly as we entered the enchanted forest, we were out of it and crisscrossing the clear, shallow waters of Nahal Dishon. In many stretches the streambed itself was the trail.

We heard the screaming before we saw them—several classes of junior-high school children stampeding through the *wadi*. Their teachers took no notice of their unruly behavior. The students charged through the water like a pack of wild dogs, running right up and deliberately splashing us. They threw each other into the stream and yelled stupid comments.

"Maybe they're a class of disturbed children," I said. "What a difference from the kids yesterday who were cleaning up the *wadi* ... and that girl who hoped to hike the trail with her husband."

"There goes our peace and quiet," said John.

We increased our pace and were thankful that we never saw them again.

We had had only a small breakfast, so after walking an hour and a half we stopped for a second breakfast. As usual when staying with people, we had packed a lunch. When we opened our packs, however, John discovered he had forgotten his sandwich, resulting in only one pita for the two of us for the rest of the day, plus a few cucumbers, tomatoes, carrots, and apples.

I have a tendency to complain, especially when there's not enough to eat, but this time I was calm. I was pleased to realize that I was able to trust God more for the little things as well as the larger ones. What good would griping do anyway?

"Never mind," I said. "we'll be eating with Steve and Rose this evening."

John smiled. "Yeah. I spoke to him on the cell phone, and he'll meet us on the trail this afternoon."

When we climbed out of Nahal Dishon we were rewarded with our first view of Mt. Hermon: a large hump reaching into the sky, its upper parts streaked with snow.

"Take a picture, Jupe!" John said as he reached for his cell phone to call the children.

We weren't far from where we expected to meet Steve, but I was feeling weak and my legs were dragging. The energy boost provided by the cucumber, orange, and granola bar for lunch had worn off.

"I need another break," I said.

We sat on a stone and shared our last granola bar.

"Steve will probably be waiting at the top of the hill where we cross the road. Just a little farther." John tried to encourage me.

When we reached the road, Steve and his car were nowhere to be seen. Although we had already hiked our daily average of nine hours, we had no choice but to keep walking. Even if we had sat and waited for Steve, we'd still have to walk back to his car with him, wherever that was. But most likely he was expecting us farther along the path.

The hill called Keren Naftali, "the horn of Naftali" loomed before us.

"Where's Steve?" I wondered aloud, as we walked across a pasture where thorny bushes and wildflowers grew between the rocks. We stepped around grazing cows and piles of manure. Soon two young men with large backpacks approached us. One called out.

"Shalom, John!"

We were startled. How did he know John?

"We're also on the *Shvil*. We met Steve, who told us to look out for John and to tell you he's waiting on the hill."

We scanned the slope ahead of us and could vaguely distinguish Steve waving his arms near the top.

"Thanks," John said. "Come to the Shelter when you finish."

The hill was steep, but at least we'd located Steve, and would soon be finishing. Keren Naftali, the highest point in the area, rewarded us with a 360-degree view from the top. After hugs and a pause to catch my breath, we began the even steeper descent.

"Look," Steve said proudly, "I took your advice and bought these walking sticks. They're great!"

*His car is probably in the parking lot at the bottom*, I thought.

However, when we reached the hill's base there was no car in sight. Steve took off striding through the fields. We had walked over an hour since our granola bar break. John and Steve chatted cheerfully in the lead, while I trailed behind.

"Hi! How are you?" I heard John call out in English.

*Who could he be speaking English to up here?* I wondered. It was nearly dark on this isolated path.

Steve's wife, Rose, dressed in red, was sitting on a rock. "You gave us an excuse to get out," she told us. "But I can't keep up with Steve, so I waited here for you." They hadn't reckoned that we had been walking the whole day already.

*Now the car must be nearby*, I reasoned to myself.

I was walking like a robot. When I tried casually several times to ask where the car was, Rose cheerfully replied, "Not far now, just around the bend."

The sun was setting over the Golan Heights, the fish ponds in the Hula Valley reflecting the blushing pink sky, when the domed ruins of Nebi Yusha appeared in the near darkness. This was the traditional Muslim site for the tomb of Joshua, the successor of Moses. As we climbed the final stone steps up to the road where Steve's car was parked, John reached down and nearly hauled me up. We'd been on the trail for 11½ hours and had walked about twenty-eight kilometers, our record day. I crumpled into the back seat of the car.

"I've prepared dinner already, and afterwards we were thinking about a game of rummy," said Rose, who is a wonderful hostess.


Amazingly I won a round of rummy, and by the next morning was completely revived and ready for our second-to-last day on the Trail. Our hike along the side of the ridge opposite the Golan Heights and above the Jordan River provided us with impressive views for nearly the entire path.

Particularly striking was Mt. Hermon, towering on our right and drawing closer as we progressed towards Kiryat Shmona. Mt. Hermon, the southern tip of the Anti-Lebanon Range—which runs east of and parallel to the Lebanon Range—is actually composed of three summits, the highest reaching 2800 meters, Syria's highest mountain. The southern and western slopes of Mt. Hermon, together with the Golan Heights to its south, came under the control of Israel in June 1967 as the result of the Six Day War. On its upper reaches in Israel is an army base; on the slopes below is Israel's only ski resort.

"Take a picture," John suggested at an especially stunning spot

where the white-topped Mt. Hermon surged above a plantation of
peach trees in full bloom.

We were soaring along in awe. "Jupe, we've walked to Kiryat
Shmona. Can you believe it?"

"Yeah, who ever walks to Kiryat Shmona from Eilat?" I
answered. "When we started out in Taba, did you think we'd
reach here?"

"I'm not sure. I can't remember anymore what I was thinking," John admitted.

While caught up in admiring the view and trekking through a
spectacular anemone-studded field, we lost the path. We weren't
paying attention to the map, and at an intersection of trails we
took the wrong arm; we followed the way that looked logical to us.
After ten minutes we noticed that we were seeing blue trail markers, but not the tri-colored Israel Trail logos. We had to backtrack
until we discovered our mistake. It seemed that no matter how
much experience we had gathered in our forty-one days of hiking,
we were always capable of going astray. We needed to maintain
a constant state of alertness and not grow lax about consulting the
map nor complacent and think we knew what we were doing.

In my spiritual walk I also have to keep vigilant, not become
overly confident or proud, or I'll be setting myself up for a
departure from the correct path and for a fall. The book of
Proverbs, a book of wisdom, speaks often about choosing correct
paths and ways. "Let your eyes look straight ahead, fix your gaze
directly before you. Make level paths for your feet and take only
ways that are firm. Do not swerve to the right or the left; keep
your foot from evil." This was our goal on our trek, but even more
so on our journey through life.

After a wide circle in a forest around the town of Kiryat
Shmona, the largest city in the upper Galilee, we ended our hike
for the day in *Kibbutz* Kfar Giladi. We spent a few minutes
reading the signs near the Tel Hai museum, whose stockade and

watchtower are connected with the Israeli hero, Josef Trumpledor.

Born in Russia, Trumpledor lost an arm while a soldier in the czar's army. In 1912 he immigrated to Palestine and fought with the World War I British troops in Gallipoli, the European part of Turkey. After the war he returned to Palestine and established the northern settlement of Tel Hai where he lived with a small, dedicated group of pioneers. After three years of living in peace with their Arab neighbors, they were betrayed and eight of the settlers, including Trumpledor, were murdered. Trumpledor is famous for his reported last words, "It is good to die for our country."

I have always felt a special kinship with Tel Hai, because my Israeli uncle, Dr. Gary, was the attending doctor to whom Trumpledor uttered this legendary sentence.

Josh, our son, and Hanan, who had walked the Nazareth section with us, had said they'd like to join us on our last day, but in the end we walked alone. Perhaps it was fitting. We enjoyed having others traveling with us, but we did best as a couple. We had heard about *Shvil* groups breaking up because they couldn't get along. Others stayed together but drifted apart after they finished. One young man told us, speaking of a former fellow-hiker, "I can't even stand his smell."

After thirty years of marriage we knew each other better than we knew anyone else on the planet, but as a result of this journey, our relationship had developed in special ways. Although I had hoped to tread every kilometer of the *Shvil*, I had learned not to be a stickler, not to drive John crazy if we missed a kilometer or two here or there. And he understood that when I was really tired or hungry I had to stop immediately before I collapsed. We walked at the same pace, were interested in the same things along the way, and liked to eat the same food.

In fact, as we began our final day on the Trail, a twelve-kilometer segment from Tel Hai to Kibbutz Dan, we were celebrating our thirtieth wedding anniversary. When we first had the vision to walk the Trail, or when we began hiking two months previously, we never could have engineered it to finish on this special day. But since we couldn't organize such perfect timing, we felt that God had. And Georgi, a friend from Switzerland, had arranged for us to stay at the guest house of his friend, Itzik, in Neve Ativ, the tourist village on the slopes of Mt. Hermon. It would be a fitting celebration for the end of our trek and for our anniversary.

With mixed feelings we set off from Tel Hai, elated to be completing the project we had embarked upon, but also sorry to have no more Trail stretching ahead of us. A few distinctive tri-colored markers led us across the square, with its famous lion statue commemorating the massacre of Trumpledor and his friends, and into a field overgrown with mustard plants.

Within five minutes we had totally lost all traces of our trail logo. They were evidently covered over by the shoulder-high yellow flowers. We weren't actually lost, thanks to our map and to the fact that we could see in the distance the road we were supposed to cross. John was delighted to have another possibility to bushwhack.

We were walking in the "Finger of the Galilee," so called because it points like a finger between the Golan Heights to the east, the rest of Israel to the south, and Lebanon to the west and north. The waters of the Jordan River originate high in the snowfields of Mt. Hermon. At the mountain's base the water gushes out in three springs which become the three tributaries of the Jordan: Dan, Hermon, and Snir.

After crossing a bridge over the road, we entered the Snir Nature Reserve. The trail soon descended into the flowing waters of the *nahal*. A trail sign was painted on a rock under the water, so this time even John was obligated to remove his boots, though we both put them on again immediately afterwards. Between the thick reeds and willows growing along the *wadi*'s banks, we nearly bumped into two girls with hiking boots dangling from their large backpacks.

"Shalom, shalom!" they called out, excited to meet us. We had likewise hoped—and prayed—to meet Israel Trail hikers on our last day.

"We just started a few hours ago, but plan to hike the whole trail," Liraz told us.

"We got a bit lost in the beginning, around the *kibbutz*," Ronit smiled sheepishly.

Their questions gushed out like the waters of the stream. "What about water in the south? Did you walk the new sections or the old?"

This was our first encounter with two girls hiking the Trail alone. "How about a picture with us three girls?" I asked John. With their wide grins, Ronit and Liraz looked so young and fresh and full of expectation.

John and I glanced at the water in front of us, trying to decide whether it was worth removing our shoes.

"You may as well take off your boots—you'll be coming to a lot of water from now on," Liraz said.

I happily unzipped my pant legs and put on my waterproof sandals, the first time I had done so since we began our hike. Till now I'd used them as slippers in the evening after we stopped walking.

"My boots are already soaked," said John, "so I might as well keep them on." John's boots, new when we started, were falling apart and had become waterlogged when he'd slipped off a rock on a previous crossing.

The trail plowed straight through the stream. We slogged through water up to our knees, trying not to stumble on the stones in the riverbed nor catch our packs on the thorny bushes along the edges. It was difficult but beautiful, with the gurgling stream, huge plane trees above us nearly blocking all sunlight, and ferns, laurel, and brambles on the riverbanks.

In a small clearing next to the *nahal*, we met a young couple, their large backpacks leaning against some trees. Seeing the man in the water inspired John to strip down to his shorts and jump in too.

"Hey! It's not really that cold," John called back. As he tried to swim to the other side without getting swept downstream by the current, I approached the hikers.

"How about a cup of coffee?" they offered, taking out their little gas stove.

We had plenty of time, and as far as I was concerned, the later we finished, the better. Today we weren't in a hurry.

"We started the Israel Trail today," the young man told us.

The girl took out a cigarette and lit up. "We'll see how far we get before it becomes too hot. We're going slowly in the beginning to get in shape."

Trekking through the moving stream was challenging, but at one point we were aided by a chicken-wire fence along the side. Gripping the wire mesh with our fingers, we pulled ourselves up the burbling brook.

Just a few meters beyond the fence stood wooden platforms supporting tables exquisitely set with tablecloths and wine glasses. This was the well-known restaurant Dag al-Hadan, or Fish-on-the-Dan, famous for its fresh-caught trout. The tempting smell of grilled fish wafted our way.

"Isn't it about time for our lunch break?" I asked John.

"Here?! In the middle of the *wadi*?" he answered. "Let's get onto dry ground first."

Exiting the park, we were soon hiking on a dirt road through a wildflower-studded field, when in front of us a large sign appeared:

*Stop! Border in Front of You*

We had begun our journey one hundred meters from the Egyptian border, and now we had reached the Lebanese border.

"Can you believe it?" John exclaimed. "Take a picture!"

I gazed with longing over the sign into Lebanon. If there were peace in our region, then we could keep hiking northward.

The trail dipped occasionally from a flat, rocky cattle range into the luxuriant, dense reeds of the *nahal*. The cows evidently used the same paths as we did to cross the stream, muddying the water. Frogs croaked loudly.

All too soon we were walking along the perimeter fence of Tel Dan Nature Reserve, the ruins of a city set on a hill surrounded by lush greenness. Dan, one of the largest and most important cities in the ancient world, was built at the intersection of two major trade routes and encompassed three springs. Its extensive excavations include imposing walls and gates, and a pagan altar that may have been the shrine on which King Jeroboam of Israel sacrificed to one of his golden calves.

A sign nearby read *Beit Ussishkin*, the archaeological and nature museum which marked the Trail's beginning, or end. Tears came to my eyes.

"Look, the sign," I stammered.

"Yeah." John didn't get it.

I couldn't explain my feelings upon seeing the name printed next to the Israel Trail symbol.

"That's it—the end—we're here."

We walked quietly, reverently, down the driveway to the stone building. Next to the parking lot was the Trail board with its maps, and written across the top: *Dan (Beit Ussishkin)*. That was all. No balloons, fireworks, or welcoming committee. John and I were alone in front of our final white, blue, and orange logo. We looked around. A woman was working in the office of the museum. We were both drawn to her.

"We just finished the Trail," John announced. "After forty-two days walking from Eilat."

She had undoubtedly met many people who could make the same boast, yet she seemed impressed. "Well done!" she said.

"Have many people finished here lately?" I wanted to know.

"No, we see more who are starting their hike here," she replied. "In fact, two girls started today, and two hours later they wandered by again. They got lost in the *kibbutz*."

We wandered over to a picnic table and started phoning our children. "We finished!"

A girl with a large pack came running up to us. "The woman in the office told me you just finished the Trail," she exclaimed. "I've been hearing about you and even saw one of your flyers. I've been walking behind you."

I wondered what she'd heard. About an old couple with poles who believed in Jesus?

"You traveled alone?" I asked.

"Friends joined me, but the last one left a few hours ago."

We hugged each other. This girl, Hela, alone at the finish, was thrilled to be able to share her victory with others who understood.

A busload of Ethiopian immigrant teenagers pulled up to the museum.

"Can you take a picture of the three of us?" John asked the twenty-something man who was giving orders to the rest.

Our phone rang. "I just came off the mountain, finished work for the day," Itzik said. "I'm waiting for you at home. Tomorrow I'll take you up to the top of Hermon."

We slung our packs on our backs and walked out to the road to begin our hitchhike up the hill to Neve Ativ, the *moshav* and holiday village. Our last night. Our anniversary. Tomorrow we'd be going home.

# 16. Can't Stop Walking

Itzik's guest house looked like a Swiss chalet. Wood paneling, thick comforters on the beds, lovely decor in the room, and the cool mountain air made us feel we'd been transported to the Alps. The perfect spot for a romantic thirtieth wedding anniversary!

John was eager to go up to Mt. Hermon to see the snow. I had seen plenty of snow in my life, and at this point, still involved in an active lifestyle, I preferred to ski in snow rather than just look at it. After forty-two days of trekking through Israel, to ascend the mountain on the non-skiers chairlift seemed tame and touristy to me. However, John was so keyed up and determined that I couldn't help but agree. Anyway, I wasn't ready to go home yet; I welcomed any excuse to prolong our journey.

"You can drive with me up to the ski lodge at the mountain's base when I go to work in the morning," Itzik offered, "and I'll put you on the chairlift." He was a manager of the ski area.

So at 8 A.M. the next day we found ourselves on our way up to the snow, calling this our "bonus day." As we had observed from a distance two days earlier on the Trail, the only snow left was on the peak, so the ski slopes were already closed for the season.

"Don't worry about getting us down," John told Itzik. "We'll walk."

On the lift ride to the top station, John was like a child at the circus. "See! Aren't you glad we're here?!" he exclaimed.

The chair lift passed through a cold clammy mist, and when we stepped out of the building at the top, I quickly put on my stocking cap. Yet here the sun shone dazzlingly. We were standing in white snowfields interrupted by rough brown rocks.

We should have had views as far as Damascus in Syria and to the Mediterranean Sea, but as we stared into the distance, all we could see were fluffy clouds. The top of Mt. Hermon was floating above a billowy white sea.

Mt. Hermon is the third possible site for the Mount of Transfiguration. Some biblical scholars claim that it is historically and geographically more suitable than Mt. Tabor or Mt. Meron. The Bible tells us that Jesus led his disciples "up a high mountain." Mt. Tabor, the traditional site, could not really be called a high mountain, except in relation to the area around it. We had ascended all three candidates. Jesus and His three disciples—Peter, James, and John—would have had a time-consuming and strenuous hike up Mt. Hermon. On the other hand, being here on such a day, feeling that we were detached from the rest of the world below us, I could easily imagine a bright cloud enveloping them, and a voice from the cloud speaking.

I swallowed hard and my throat felt tight with emotion. "Here we are at the highest point and most northern point in Israel, and tonight we'll be home in Eilat."

"Yeah," John agreed. "Can you believe it's over?"

"We'll ask one of the lift operators to take our picture," he added, looking around. "Let's stand in front of that huge snow drift with the clouds behind us and our poles in the air."

"I hope we'll be able to walk in the snow." I was skeptical. "What if the snow's really wet and heavy, or too deep?"

We posed for the camera, then headed down one of the ski slopes, surprised to find the snow was not too slushy or crunchy. Traversing and sliding down the snowfields, using our poles for balance, we felt alternately like Alpine explorers and ski-less skiers.

After an hour of sliding we reached the ski lodge and had a cup of coffee in the sun with Itzik. We would have liked to hike all the way down, but most of Mt. Hermon is a closed military area. So we settled for a trek in a green, flower-filled *wadi* with a bubbling stream running through it. Our last *wadi*, our last hike.

At the end of the trail we hitched a ride back to the Fish-on-the-Dan restaurant that we had waded by the previous day. This time we sat at a table like normal diners, like tourists. While enjoying a delicious meal of trout, I kept my eye on the perimeter fence—maybe we'd see some *Shvil* hikers splashing through the water. We did hear the shouts of a school class headed downstream, falling over the rocks and over each other into the icy waters.

John told Michal, our waitress, that we had just finished the Israel Trail and that it was our thirtieth wedding anniversary. To our surprise, along with the after-dinner tea and coffee we ordered, she brought us an ice cream sundae with sparklers, "on the house." I blinked back my tears.

"Here, read this," John said, handing Michal a tract. "And come visit us in Eilat."

Was she the last one to receive one of our pamphlets on our trip? Would she, or others we'd met, come to the Shelter?

One of the last Israel Trail hikers we'd met had told us about attending a *Shvil* preparedness lecture in Tel Aviv and receiving a list of names of people called Trail Angels. These were people along the path of the Trail who wanted to help through-hikers in any way—by bringing them water, offering accommodation, giving advice, etc. I decided to become an "angel" and to somehow register the Shelter among the other "angels."

Perhaps this would help us to attract a new sort of client.

When we began our hostel twenty years ago, nearly all our

guests were backpackers and young travelers. But Israel has
become a relatively expensive country and people are seeking
more exotic destinations such as Vietnam and Guatemala. Today,
although we still host the twenty-somethings, many of our guests
are older or families.

The young people hiking the Trail were exactly the kind of
guests we loved having at the hostel: nature-loving, respectful of
others, enjoying interacting with different cultures. Once the word
spread that their first night was free, chances were they'd come.

For us, networking with other *Shvil* hikers would help, I
prayed, to keep the spirit of our trip alive. I hoped to remember
the lessons I'd learned from this pivotal experience—trusting God,
bringing issues and people immediately to Him in prayer, living
in the present and not worrying about the future, plus many more.
I wanted to imprint in my memory the stark desert scenery with
its infinite shades of brown and beige, red and rust, the Galilee's
lush, green, flower-studded meadows, the silence and freedom of
the outdoors, and the camaraderie with fellow walkers. We deeply
appreciated our personal trail angels and knew that we could bless
others, whether at the end or the beginning of their journey.

After our celebration we hitched back to Kiryat Shmona and
took a bus to the Tel Aviv airport. Once again we had the
opportunity to review our trip as we zipped past familiar places
on the bus.

"Look, John! Here's where we crossed the highway."

"Jupe, that's the field where we got lost."

I could imagine us driving crazy any friends or family who
happened to be in the car with us in the future, as we continuously
pointed out the *Shvil* route. Traveling through Israel would never
be the same again. We had developed an intimate connection with
the land and its geography.

I hoped to return and hike through places that had interested
us but which we weren't able to explore on this journey. Israel

has thousands of kilometers of hiking trails including many areas that the *Shvil* doesn't cover, such as the Golan Heights, Western Galilee, and the Judean Desert around the Dead Sea. Now that we had the equipment and the backpacking experience, we could make more trips through Israel ... or the world! Having begun, I knew I couldn't stop walking.

I was in a meditative mood. I knew my life would never be the same. Whatever happened after this, no one could ever take this experience away from us. Perhaps this would inspire us to take other creative breaks from our busy lives. Or we could inspire others. In Hebrew the word *nofesh* means "rest, recreation, or holiday." Interestingly, the root letters are the same as the word *nefesh* which means "soul." Jewish scholars also translate *nefesh* as "the essence of life" or "the state of being alive." Whereas the word *shvita*, in connection with the seventh day, is used for "cessation of work" and has the same root as *shabbat*, *nofesh* implies leisure in a positive sense—creative self-discovery. Walking the land had been a true rest for our souls.

While waiting for our flight, I took out my diary and wrote in it for the last time. How could I begin to evaluate all we had learned through this experience? Our forty-two days of walking were over, but I was convinced that the repercussions would extend far into the future.

At one friend's house along the way, a woman had come up to me and asked, "Why are you doing this?" By her tone she seemed to imply, "Why waste your time?"

So I made a list to sum up our motives:

- *A break, or sabbatical, from the work*
- *A chance to draw closer to God and to trust in Him in a deeper way*
- *More time to pray*

- *Time for each other*
- *Get to know the land of Israel and its beauty*
- *Renew ties with friends and congregations in the north*
- *Meet interesting people*
- *Share our faith*
- *Get exercise and fresh air*

Was our journey an escape? Maybe; but I concluded it was a focused escape. We had set goals for ourselves and had achieved them.

Our walk might stimulate people's interest in God, the Bible, and Israel. We could use a computerized slide show to share with friends and family the beauty of Israel and the experience of trekking through it. Telling our story in a book would be an enormous challenge, but at the same time it would enable us to prolong our experience and extend our message.

Our flight was announced. I grabbed my pack and poles and strode towards the gate. In an hour we'd be landing in Eilat—smiling, loving friends and family waiting for us. Our journey was over.

I had proved to myself that it's worthwhile to dream and to commit to fulfilling the dream. I learned that most anything is possible, even at our age. I wondered what would be next.

# GLOSSARY OF HEBREW & ARABIC WORDS

*Aliya* — going up; immigration to Israel
*Arava* — part of the Rift Valley between Israel and Jordan
*Carbolet* — cock's comb; crest of a mountain
*Druze* — a monotheistic religious sect living in the mountains of
　　Israel, Syria, and Lebanon
*Ein* — spring
*Gev* (plural: *gevim*) — cistern
*Har* — mountain
*Hassidim* — a sect of Orthodox Jews who follow a strict interpretation
　　of the Mosaic Law
*Hurva* — ruins
*Jalabiya* — Bedouin man's clothing
*Kef Halek* — How are you? (Arabic)
*Kibbutz* (plural: *kibbutzim*) — communal settlement
*Kibbutznik* — member of *kibbutz*
*Kippa* (plural: *kippot*) — the skullcap worn by religious Jewish men
*Lebaneh* — sour milk cheese
*Lila Tov* — Good night
*Ma'aslameh* — Good-bye (Arabic)
*Mapal* (plural: *mapalim*) — waterfall, usually dry in the south of Israel
*Mishlat* — vantage point
*Moshav* (plural: *moshavim*) — cooperative village
*Pita* (plural: *pitot*) — flat round Arab bread
*Shabbat* — Saturday, Israel's day of rest
*Shtetl* — pre-Holocaust European village with large Jewish population
*Shukran* — Thank you (Arabic)
*Shvil* — path
*Talmud* — the authoritative body of Jewish tradition
*Tel* — a mound composed of the remains of previous settlements
*Torah* — the first five books of the Bible
*Wadi* (Arabic), *Nahal* (Hebrew) — streambed, dry in the summer
*Yeshiva* — an academy for the study of Jewish texts, especially the Talmud
*Yeshua* — Jesus

To order additional copies of this book, contact your
local bookstore or visit the publisher's Web site at:
www.cladach.com
To learn about the Shelter Hostel and *Walk the Land*
in Israel, visit:
www.shelterhostel.com